CLASSIC REPRINT

FIFTY YEARS
OF FOOTBALL
1884-1934

By

SIR FREDERICK WALL

INTRODUCTION

Originally published in 1935, 'Fifty Years of Football' contains the fascinating reminiscences of Sir Frederick Wall who held the post of Secretary of the Football Association from 1895 to 1934. During this 39-year period, Sir Frederick's dedicated work led him to become one of the sport's most influential figures and these personal memoirs provide a great insight into the history and development of the game.

With original copies priced in excess of £100.00 each, this reissue as part of our *Classic Reprint* series gives football followers the opportunity to own a really important historical account of the world's favourite sport.

British Library Cataloguing in Publication Data
A catalogue record for this book is available from the British Library

ISBN 1-86223-116-8

Copyright © 2006, SOCCER BOOKS LIMITED. (01472 696226)
72 St. Peter's Avenue, Cleethorpes, N.E. Lincolnshire, DN35 8HU, England

www.soccer-books.co.uk

Printed by 4edge Ltd. www.4edge.co.uk

FIFTY YEARS OF FOOTBALL

CHAPTER I

MY EARLY DAYS

COMING from the yeomanry stock, once described as the "backbone of old England," none of my relatives would have been surprised had I maintained the family tradition as a farmer. As the old song says: "To plough and to sow, to reap and to mow, to be a farmer's boy."

Exactly; but circumstances ordered otherwise and environment was overcome. The family farmed lands in the latter part of the eighteenth and in the first half of the nineteenth century in remote parts of the south-eastern counties. My father was from Essex and my mother from Hertfordshire.

Born on April 14, 1858, one of three brothers, the country village of Battersea is my native place. The Walls had moved so as to be within easier reach of Covent Garden Market. Surprise may be expressed at the description of Battersea as a village in the country, but at that time there were only a few folk living in cottages near to several large estates.

Those were the days of the lavender fields, of market gardens, with chestnut and yew trees on the landscape. Open fields lay between the village and the wooden bridge across the Thames, near to the site of the present stone bridge. The nearest village, Wandsworth, was over the hill and approached by lanes.

At the corner of St. John's Road, as it is now called, adjacent to Lavender Hill, vegetables were loaded daily and taken on the waggons to London, and on returning the driver would pull up at the old Falcon Inn for refreshment. Outside this inn was a horse-trough, again made of wood, for thirsty horses, with a pump attached. The horse-trough is now as rare as the tape that preceded the cross-bar of the goal.

While a boy at Lordship House School, Wandsworth Common, I became a chorister at St. Mark's Church. After studying at St. Mark's College, Chelsea, early in my teens I was engaged as a junior clerk by a firm of solicitors and company lawyers, of which Sir Henry Kimber was the principal partner. There was an association football club called The Rangers, formed by the members of St. Mark's Guild, and I was chosen as honorary secretary and treasurer when seventeen years of age.

Descending from forbears who led an open-air life, games played out-of-doors appealed to me. I liked football, a pastime that was a joyous revel for the middle classes in grey autumn and early winter, just as much as is foxhunting for the wealthy in these months of chilly weather.

We were enthusiasts and played on the west side of Clapham Common, while some other boisterous young sportsmen pursued the Rugby ball on the east side of the Common. They were known as The Fireflies. But another Rugby club wished to play on the ground the Rangers usually occupied. Therefore it was my duty to be first on to the pitch we liked and put up the goal-posts and fasten the tape at the top. How many youngsters of this day erect their goal-posts?

There came a day when it was necessary to move, and we rented a field behind the house of Mr. Philip Cazenove, the stockbroker, who conducted a bible-class in his dining-room. There I met the Rev. H.B. Verdon, a curate to the vicar, the Rev. J. Erskine Clarke. Mr. Verdon was an aristocrat and a splendid type of godly athlete who once said to me: "My family came over to England with William the Conqueror and found your ancestors here on their arrival."

The Rangers became quite a good club, and it was advisable to hire another field. This was near to Wandsworth Common, adjoining the ground of The Casuals, and adjacent to the county gaol. That seemed a bit of a joke to us. We had a large number of players and a good second eleven who were winning matches. They became so cock-a-hoop that they challenged the first team, who only won by 3–1.

The Casuals used to dress at a tavern, and had to run 300 yards across the Common to their field. The Rangers had to seek dressing-room accommodation, but there was no other inn we could use. So we went cap in hand to the Wandsworth Common Church Institute, where Mr. C.H. Baker was a gentleman who devoted his life to the welfare of boys.

He welcomed us, but he made this condition—that all the Rangers should become members of the institute, enjoy its advantages and share its responsibilities. This Wandsworth Institute had a Rugby club and quite a good fifteen. They entered a competition for the Jersey Football Trophy. In 1884, they reached the final tie and their opponents were the Richmond Church Institute. Then, as now, Richmond was a Rugby stronghold. The Richmond Club was nineteen years old and gained great prestige by the aid of the Gurdons, whose surname has not lost its lustre, even after fifty years, among those with a long life.

It was rumoured that some of the Richmond players were qualified to play for the Richmond Church Institute and would do so. The Wandsworth secretary anticipated defeat and asked for help by the Rangers. I said: "There is nothing we should revel in more. How many do you want?" "We would like three fast men," he answered. I replied, "All right." Charlie Miller and Bob Read, two of our fastest forwards, volunteered, and I thought I would like to play. We all did.

Young, strong and rather fast, I was placed at three-quarter back in order to stop some of the other fellows. One of these hefty Richmond Rugby men came tearing through. I felt perplexed. Any Association tackle would be hopeless. I jumped at him and flinging my arms round the lower part of the thighs I brought him down.

Clearly that was the game. This gave me more confidence and I managed to scramble through the match.

The Wandsworth Institute won, and we all received a medal in the shape of a tiny shield. This had no intrinsic worth, for it was neither gold nor silver but just copper, and probably of the value of twopence, apart from its splendid workmanship. I sometimes look at this souvenir and laugh at my adventure in the Rugby game.

From Wandsworth we again had to trek and make way for the house-builders. The Rangers seemed rightly named. We went to Hasking's Sports Ground, near Balham railway station. Before closing my recollections of the Rangers I should like to say that the club entered for the Football Association Cup, so that we might have the opportunity of playing against a crack eleven.

In 1880–81 we had a bit of luck. The Wanderers scratched to us, and in the second round we received a bye. There are no byes in these fierce times, and no club dreams of scratching. In the third round we were drawn against the Royal Engineers, who were quite at their best. This was a red-letter entry in our calendar.

We met them at Kennington Oval and were very well beaten by 6–0. We enjoyed every minute of the match, inasmuch as we had played against such a famous team on the classic ground at Kennington.

And I prepared for the match by having a good rump steak for lunch. That will shock the modern trainer, who believes in a light lunch for his team at least two hours before the kick-off... In ancient days we were not so finicking, for football was then just a game.

A system of raising funds, such as that favoured by league clubs, had never been dreamed of. Our teams were drawn from local players who paid their annual subscriptions and their own expenses for travel and outfit. There were some honorary members who gave donations to satisfy the landlord. The Rangers, who became the oldest club in East or Mid-Surrey, with the exception of the Clapham Rovers, could go through a season, with two matches each Saturday, on an expenditure of about £30, and then have a balance in hand of nearly £4.

That is the way a sound and thoroughly genuine amateur club used to fare about fifty years ago. Those who manage amateur clubs in this era will be able to make comparison. And no set of players could have got more sport and enjoyment out of the game than did we of the Rangers. A small club? Yes, but large and expensive families are not always the happiest, are they?

I was not a man of one sport without interest in any other game. As a member of the Remex Rowing Club, I rowed in the "eights" and the "four-oars," at cricket my slow over-arm bowling was the means of dismissing six men for 26 runs in an inter-regimental match. With two other members of the Rangers, when eighteen years of age I joined the Seventh Surrey Rifles, whose headquarters were at Kennington Lane. One of the Beresfords was our lieutenant-colonel. In two years my rank was that of a sergeant.

This is one side of life; the active physical side during early manhood. Let us turn to another, that throws more light upon the administrative aspect of football. After five years with Sir Henry Kimber I took up a position with Mr. J. Brend Batten, a Devonshire gentleman, who was a solicitor and parliamentary agent in Westminster. This firm developed into Messrs. Batten, Proffitt and Scott, and I remained with them until appointed secretary to the Football Association.

For years all my leisure was devoted to the governing and ordering of football. This phase began with the Rangers and was continued for thirteen years, from 1875 to 1888. I became a member of the council of the London Football Association in 1881, was attached to the Rules Revision and Emergency Committees, and was elected a vice-president in 1892. Taking an active interest in the Middlesex County Association in 1888, I was appointed Honorary Secretary and Treasurer in 1890.

Middlesex was reorganized and grew into the largest and one of the most prosperous of kindred bodies, and I represented the county on the Football Association from 1891. In this year there were three members of the Council who are still in office, namely, Mr. J.C. Clegg (now Sir Charles), elected in 1886, Mr. W.

Pickford, elected in 1888, and Mr. A.G. Hines, elected in 1889, and they came respectively from the Sheffield, Hampshire and Notts Associations.

Four years later Mr. C.W. Alcock, of the Old Harrovians, who was the Secretary of the parent Association, resigned. There were upwards of 200 applicants for the position, myself included. I had not thought of doing so, but Mr. J. Mark McDonnell, a solicitor, who was for many years my colleague when with Mr. Batten, suggested I should apply, as he considered that my experience in sport and in law would prove useful.

A committee reduced the applicants to three, who were to be interviewed by the Council. They were Mr. Fred Bye, a prominent leader of the game at Sheffield, Mr. James Grant, who was identified with the Liverpool and District Association, and myself. I was appointed by a majority of three votes.

I should like to add that my application had the support of Sir Francis Marindin, R.E., formerly President of the F.A. and ex-chairman of the Council. This famous Old Etonian, then Inspecting Officer of Railways to the Board of Trade, wrote to say that he thought I was "very well fitted" for the post. Perhaps his letter turned the scale. Thus in 1895, at thirty-seven years of age, I started upon a new career in the offices then at Chancery Lane, the staff consisting of one junior clerk.

The first duty was to reorganize the office arrangements and general system of working, and to get a diploma as a Fellow of the Chartered Institute of Secretaries, solely with the object of the knowledge being helpful. At this time letters had to be written by hand. There are now other methods of producing letters, and without latter-day inventions a large staff would have been required to keep abreast of the expansion of Association football, which has changed from a British game played by the few, to a world game played by millions.

The change in England alone has been tremendous. In 1895 there were 44 members of the Council of the Football Association, which had 188 clubs in direct membership. Now there are 78 councillors and thousands more clubs, although only 200 are fully qualified members, since for some years the Associations have only admitted the premier clubs of the different counties. Of course, these figures do not include 73 affiliated associations with tens of thousands of clubs and hundreds of thousands of players.

The Football Association have a world-wide organization embracing not only all parts of the British Empire, but places like Tientsin and Shanghai. Few folks have any idea of the growth of the game, and still fewer any conception of the work the parent body has done to encourage the sport in all countries and among all peoples irrespective of creed and colour.

I say this because the Association has been charged with being insular and therefore narrow-minded. At Chancery Lane in 1895, there was, perhaps, an attitude that England was our parish and that we had no liabilities to the game in other countries. With the aid of enthusiastic assistants and the pick of English professionals we soon began to take a wider view. The F.A. have done much missionary work since 1899. This has been carried out in our own way and in accord with our own ideas.

I am expressing these views in order to show that the F.A. have done great missionary work overseas and that we have kept abreast of modern movements while preserving our independence of thought and action.

The advance of football in England may be shown, in one way, by the finances of the F.A. When I became Secretary over 39 years ago, the entire assets were £8,145. Our last financial statement showed that the assets were £149,535, and of this sum £101,663 represented investments. This money has come to the Association since the war. Between 1914–18 our funds vanished. We were glad of help from any quarter.

How do I account for this extraordinary accretion of funds? It is due to the general growth and popularity of the game, the revenue from international matches and the percentages upon "gates" in our Cup competitions, mainly from the Final and Semi-Final ties for the Association Challenge Cup. No one can say what the F.A. will do with their accumulated funds, but from what has happened during my time, the inference that thought and care will still be exercised over expenditure seems justified.

It has been my pleasure to see the game attain a popularity that is almost universal. I do wish, however, that we had football of the type that was seen in 1895—the year that must serve me as a starting point for these retrospects. The style of play has been changed. Was it not delightful to have the forwards coming along as a line, passing to one another? We used to have the half-backs "feeding" their forwards, who worked out an attack and scored. They would keep the ball at their feet under control, and when they passed they passed accurately.

What is present-day football? I venture to say that the Corinthians are responsible for the change in the style of play. The man at the back of the Corinthians was N. Lane Jackson, perhaps better known to most people as "Pa" Jackson. I can hear him now, shouting out at matches, "First time!" Volleying the ball, taking it on the half-volley, and kicking it or shooting without the fraction of a second in delay—that is slap-dash football.

The slap-dash manner seldom pays in any walk of life. You don't find players getting the ball under command and sending it accurately to whom they wish. It is "first time," and if they succeed with such a touch it is more by luck than judgment that an accurate pass is made to the player for whom it was intended. The style at the present time does not appeal to me as did that of my early days.

Let us get back to first principles, meaning control of the ball and more accuracy in using it to the advantage of the side. No doubt many will call this the view of an old man who lives in the past. But I don't. In this era speed is generally the first consideration. I prefer skill with the foot.

And I dislike intensely this bonus system. Pay the player well.

It should be very plainly understood that whilst the club fulfil their part of the bargain, it is the duty of players to give of their best at all times, and to play the game as sportsmen both on and off the field. By all means pay professionals well for good service, but let there be no payment or offer of bonus in advance for a win or a draw.

When England played Italy at Rome last May the Italians were receiving very large wages; three or four times higher than the wages paid in England. We were informed that Signor Mussolini promised that if they won they should have in addition to their wages a bonus of £16 per man. They did not win. They drew. We were told that even then Mussolini was so pleased that he authorized the payment of £16 to each man. What did our boys think?

I hold that it was a mistake ever to have introduced bonuses, whether in England, Italy, or anywhere else. The Football Association have never paid a bonus. They once tried, without the least concealment, to raise the standard fee for international matches, but as other British countries were unable to pay as much, the idea was not persevered with.

CHAPTER II

CALLERS—WELCOME AND OTHERWISE

No sooner had I been installed in the Chancery Lane offices than it became clear that I was not merely a "post-card writer," as Tom Watson, the canny Northumbrian, who was the secretary of the Liverpool club, used to say in describing some of his brethren occupying the same kind of position. All sorts and conditions of men call upon the administrative officials of the F.A. They always have done and always will.

In my early days a club manager of the old school came to see me. At that time urgency registration of players who were professionals had not been introduced. No man who had been signed on a form for registration was eligible to take part in a match until the club had received from the F.A. a certificate that this had been done.

The form relating to one of these transactions was posted in Lancashire on the Friday and could not reach me before the match was played. Nevertheless, the Lancashire manager included his recruit in the team. There was trouble because the young man was not qualified. The manager travelled to London especially to persuade me to say that the form had been received in time, and that I had issued the certificate in time for the player to be eligible.

Although I was the young secretary I could not see the wisdom of putting my head into a noose. I was not able to do as he wished. I was not going to tell a lie. Some of the managers of long ago were inclined to be fox-headed.

How different was the action of Mr. John McKenna, the

President of the Football League and one of the vice-presidents of the Football Association. He came to me over thirty years ago. Mr. McKenna was then a director of the Liverpool club, and I had never before met him. He told me that he wanted to engage a Woolwich Arsenal player, and was going to Plumstead for the purpose. By arrangement I met him on his return. He had completed the forms and I gave him the certificate. Everything turned out as wished. Mr. McKenna has never forgotten the transaction. This was the procedure of an honest man whom it was a pleasure to oblige.

The Football Association removed from Chancery Lane to High Holborn and then to 42, Russell Square. Some people have said that "No. 42" was a haunted house. That was nonsense but these premises, which we held on lease from the trustees of the British Museum, became a store-house for the Football Battalion of the 17th Middlesex during the war. All the rooms, even the Council Chamber, were packed with supplies for the regiment. With the co-operation of voluntary helpers a great and good work was done for the men at the Western front.

The Association lost all its money, but we had friends and formed committees, and I occupied myself with organizing and managing, collecting and despatching, the building serving the purpose of a depot.

Still, we might have lost the premises. We nearly did. They were commandeered in 1914 to be used for the purposes of the War Office. The authorities had the right to take possession because the building was not indispensable. The professional side of football had been closed down. I was holding the fort and looking after comforts for the battalions that had been raised. Two surveyors from the department of the Office of Works inspected "No. 42." Then three officers came and went over the building. They praised the Council Chamber and the Committee Rooms. They said that the premises were just what they were needing for war purposes. "Yes," said one of the officers, "but where's the bath?"

Of course, every place was a store-room filled with thousands of pairs of socks, tons of cigarettes and many other necessaries and comforts. I was the Honorary Secretary, and I got into touch with

Lord Derby and made representations to him that there were other houses, equally as good, in Russell Square without disturbing our work for the troops.

The officers were persistent. They asked when we were going to give up possession. I sat tight. I was then living at West Norwood, and I received a telegram that some men had taken possession and had started to pull up the drains. I got into communication with the Office of Works, and during the morning, while the men were getting on with their job, an official came and told me that he had ordered them to stop, and that we should not have any further trouble. We were left in peace because we were doing so much good work.

There are many men who wish to take advantage of the popularity of football. They ask us to make collections at every match on a certain day for this or that cause. Some people appear to think that the Football Association should be universal providers and helpers, just because we have assisted directly and indirectly so many philanthropic institutions, agencies and causes.

Other men wish to use the game for the purposes of advertisement or to obtain its patronage. Business houses have written offering to give prizes; in some cases, obviously the idea was publicity, but all received a courteous reply declining the offer. We could not accept any gift for trade purposes. There is a regulation which reads: "A competition must not be used for trade or advertising purposes, nor may the name of the donor of a cup or other trophy form part of the title of a competition."

Numerous letters are received from the inventors of new types of football, of valves and bladders, of devices for dispensing with lacing the ball, of watches for timekeeping and of ideas for football paraphernalia. Of course their object is to obtain an expression of opinion favourable to their invention or merchandise. If we deem the application likely to be of national interest the matter is carefully considered.

I was asked to referee the first women's football match at Crouch End. I declined, but I went to see the match and came to the conclusion that the game was not suitable for them. Someone declared that one of the players was a "Tommy" made up as a woman. The Football Association have discouraged this invasion of the "eternal feminine," just as they have discountenanced Sunday football.

For many years, in the suburbs of large cities and towns, Sunday league football has been played. This has been organized chiefly by public-houses. Now the London County Council has decided to permit organized football in the public parks. I shall be surprised if the F.A. do not enforce the rule that matches shall not be played within their jurisdiction on Sundays and that any person who takes part in Sunday football in the United Kingdom shall not be recognized by the Association.

Someone has always some proposition to advance in connection with football. It is one way of seeking either popularity or notoriety. There are many dangerous aspects of a great game such as ours, and the Association, always considering themselves the trustees and guardians of the sport, have acted as such. In the autumn of 1905 two men, who were carrying on a business in Birmingham, called The National Football Agency, took steps to form a football team to tour Germany and Austria. The Association did not approve of such a project, as it was conceived by private individuals for personal profit in violation of a principle that governs the game under our jurisdiction. Moreover, we have never approved of football agents in any way.

Accordingly a warning was issued to players, who were told that if they went on tour with a private firm they were not likely to be registered by us or reinstated without a vote of the Council. Nevertheless the tour was carried out and players suspended. Charles Athersmith, the international outside right of Aston Villa, a fast and clever forward, came under the ban and two amateurs were declared professionals.

A still more serious attempt to carry on the game on a private hippodrome basis was made a short time afterwards. I was approached by Mr. E. Cleary, who had drawn up a scheme to play matches indoors with artificial lighting at Olympia, London. He prepared to arrange for several teams drawn from players who were about to close their active career and youngsters who were on the threshold and would "fall" for the salary offered. He was at once told that the Association would not sanction such a circus performance; neither clubs nor players would be allowed to participate.

Mr. Cleary explained that the lighting would be improved and that he proposed to spend some thousands of pounds upon the manufacture of an artificial grass mat that would cover the space of a football pitch. As emphatically as I could, I stated that the governing body would never approve of such a plan, that the players would tender themselves liable to suspension and that he was likely to lose heavily.

The promoter paid no heed to the warning. His grass mat, said to have involved an expenditure of £5,000, was made, and his games were played. Financially the experiment was a big failure, and the players had their little troubles.

It must not be assumed from these facts that the F.A. are opposed even to indoor football, when carried out by recognized clubs under proper conditions, particularly if for a charitable object. About fifty years ago the Notts County and Nottingham Forest clubs played once a season a match in one of the largest hails in their city. Where necessary parts of the hall were covered with netting; the playing area was not quite of full size and the members of each eleven wore light shoes with indiarubber soles.

This was not a violent game but it was pretty, and was managed by two historic clubs and keen rivals who, I believe, gave the entire proceeds to one of the institutions in the city. Obviously, that is entirely another story, but it is more—an example.

When Brigadier-General Critchley, M.P., was considering ways and means to enhance the attractions of his Stadium at the White City, London, he sought my opinion with regard to a new proposal. He desired to arrange for a World's Championship of Association Football to be decided at the Stadium. He had already communicated with clubs on the Continent and in South America. Perhaps the tournament for the World's Championship Cup, which had taken place at Monte Video, under the auspices of the

Fédération Internationale, had fired his imagination.

I had to tell the Brigadier that the F.A. would never sanction such a competition, and that the other governing bodies in Britain would probably follow our example; that the same attitude would also be taken up by Imperial bodies affiliated to us; further, that Great Britain would be supported by the countries attached to the Fédération Internationale, as they generally agreed with England. General Critchley told me plainly that he was prepared to face such difficulties if they presented themselves. He may have been disappointed at the possibility of being unable to get authorization, but he was determined to proceed with his arrangements. There is always something of this kind being put forward.

Again, if we had allowed Tottenham Hotspurs to play First Vienna in Paris during November, 1933, we should have created stupendous difficulties for ourselves. Under the conditions arranged the game was ostensibly for charitable objects, but there was the probability of the receipts being swallowed up by the expenses. If one of our clubs wishes to play on the Continent they must first write to us and enable us to guard the interests of the game as well as the teams. We must be satisfied that the club abroad has a recognized status. I have learned that some outside agencies arrange Continental tours and are paid out of the profits. A French firm not only claims to arrange matches for French clubs, but boasts that it has all the best clubs of other European countries as clients. Yet the Fédération Internationale forbids the playing of matches arranged by private individuals for speculative purposes, or the payment of any percentage of the receipts to organizations or persons for any services rendered in connection with them.

When professionalism was legalized in England there were members of the Council of the F.A. who believed that it would not be wise to legislate for this new development. The Council consisted of amateurs without experience. Yet there were others who foresaw dangers of many kinds unprovided for, and visualized clubs playing outside the pale of the Association. Uncontrolled professionalism is the bane of any sport. The game has been firmly controlled in England. That has helped to ensure the popularity of the sport.

Clubs cannot do just as they like—even if they desire flood-light football. That may be in the future; I cannot predict in an era when the sorcerers of science may as easily turn night into day as they now talk to a man on the other side of the world.

Some of my visitors have not been difficult to deal with. A few years ago the Mayor of a provincial town came to see me in reference to the case of a local player. He brought with him a long petition signed by a large number of the supporters of the club. They pleaded for leniency. The man was an exceedingly good player, but his temperament was not exactly suited to the game.

I took it upon myself to show the Mayor the report of the referee. The player had spoken to this official in a manner that was not polite, or even deferential. The Mayor read the report, walked to the fireplace, put the petition on the fire and returned home a wiser and sadder man.

Players have often come to see me and sought my advice. I have always tried to put them at their ease and been as fatherly as the circumstances permitted. There are not only good players but good fellows in every team. They have generally taken my advice, and have been loyal to the spirit of the game and to their club.

I have interviewed suspicious characters. A person who said he was a player named George Simpson, and at one time the outside left of Sheffield Wednesday, wrote to me. He said that he played in the Final tie for the Association Cup at the Crystal Palace and that he had headed the winning goal against Everton. Unfortunately, his gold medal had been stolen and he would like to be given another medal in its place. This was a serious matter, because the gold medal presented to each player in the team that wins the Cup is the most cherished emblem in our national game.

I made enquiries and found that Simpson played a great part in the game, that he had started the movement which led up to the Wednesday's first goal and that he eventually won the game. But was this the real Simpson?

With the object of answering this question I asked him to come and see me. He did not appeal to me as one who had been a first-class professional and I said that I would make enquiries and let him know. I was able to get in touch with the genuine George Simpson, who still had his medal. On further enquiry I discovered that the person who had applied for the medal and told me a fairy tale was a shoeblack, or filled some such menial position, at a public school in the West of England.

I asked myself why he wanted the medal and I came to the conclusion that he wished to use it as a means of obtaining a better situation, because it would have shown that he was respectable and a man of some ability. I never troubled about what became of him.

One day when we were at Russell Square I happened to be in the clerk's office when a big Scotsman walked in. He introduced himself as a famous Scottish international who had played against England. Let us call him "Sandy," of McGilpie. He said that he had lost all his money in London and wanted to get "awa' hame" and could I lend him his railway fare to McGilpie? He had an honest, sonsie face. At least I thought so, and lent him the money. But it never came back.

I have had visitors from all parts of the Dominions and of all nationalities, of all stations in life, from a King to a peasant. I got in touch with the King of Afghanistan, Amanullah, and invited him, his Queen and their suites to visit Wembley and see a match between England and Scotland. This could not be done without approaching persons of high position, not only on King Amanullah's staff, but secretaries and equerries to our own Royal Family, as well as officials at the Foreign Office. There were no serious obstacles. These distinguished Orientals came and were delighted with the game. King Amanullah conferred on me the Order of the Star of Afghanistan, but I never got it, as there was a revolution and the King had to abdicate.

CHAPTER III

THREE GREAT PIONEERS

ASSOCIATION football owes a great deal to a man of French descent, to a sporting Scot who might be described as the Red Earl of Perthshire, and to an honest lawyer from Sheffield. Three amateurs, who successively became Presidents of the Football Association. Not one of them was a mere ornament. They played our winter game because they loved it, they worked for the spread of this manly pastime because they felt that there was none better in winter, and they schemed to hand on a great inheritance that everyone might enjoy, whether he had been to Eton or an elementary school—a recreation that aroused the Saxon's love of a fight under rules. That bit of combativeness in us can never be killed.

The first of these three famous pioneers and leaders was Sir Francis Marindin, descended from a Huguenot family who escaped to England after the St. Bartholomew business. He was President of the F.A. from a 1874 to 1890. The second we knew as Lord Kinnaird, who filled the position from 1890 to 1923, and the third is Sir Charles Clegg, who became a member of the Council in 1886, and was the successor to Lord Kinnaird when he passed over to the Elysian fields. These men should be enshrined in our memories.

Few can remember, as I do, Sir Francis Marindin. In my youth he was Major Marindin of the Royal Engineers. Everyone referred to him as "The Major," and some of the professionals, in the early days, seemed to think that they were funny when they called him "The Majaw." Marindin was an aristocrat and all that, but by no means a dandy or a la-de-da fellow. As a boy he learned to love "footer" at Eton, and he went through "the shop" at Woolwich with such honours that he was awarded a commission in the Royal Engineers. At Chatham in 1866 Marindin founded the football club of the Royal Engineers. They played on "The Lines" and won the Association Cup upon their third appearance in the Final tie. That team of 1875 was jolly strong.

By the way, shortly after Arsenal had defeated Huddersfield in the Final of 1930, I received a letter from Maj.-Gen. Sir. R.M. Ruck, who wrote: "The recent finely contested struggle for the Association Cup has reminded me that I was one of the team of Royal Engineers who won The Cup in 1875, and that I have nothing to show for it. I am nearly 79 and should be glad to leave some memento to my family. I write therefore on the chance that the Association may bestow medals on past winners, before medals were in vogue." And the Major-General, who was a lieutenant in 1875, wrote a firm first-class hand upon the note-paper of the Junior United Service Club, London. The Association were unable to comply with his request. The decision seems unfortunate.

The Royal Engineers did more than carry off our little Cup of those days. At that time Marindin was a tall, well-built, broad-shouldered back. Clever and shrewd he was. The Sappers moved in unison. They were the first English eleven to show the advantages of combination over the old style of individualism. In 1873 the Royal Engineers made the first football tour on record, as they arranged and played matches at Nottingham, Derby and Sheffield. I have often heard Sir Charles Clegg say that these "Sappers" were the first to show the value of combination in Sheffield, and the late Sam Weller Widdowson, when he was on the Council, was equally emphatic about the benefit of their example at Nottingham.

However, to return to Marindin, who was elected to the Committee of the F.A. in 1869, I have been told that when he became the chairman he was both discreet and business-like. The few who can recall him will remember his commanding figure as a referee, a capacity in which he excelled. Players might joke about "The Majaw" behind his back, but they knew his eyes were keen, that he was a fine and experienced player, and that he was a thought-reader. They dreaded his frown. When he said: "If you do that again, I shall send you off the field," they knew that he would. He did control.

Preston North End might have been bruised and sore after their Cup tie with the Old Carthusians in March, 1887, but when they turned up at Nottingham three days later to play West Bromwich Albion in their ever-memorable semi-final, they never uttered one word of complaint against "The Majaw." With what perfect self-possession he ruled that semi-final, when the Albion gained such a decisive triumph over the "Invincibles," as the Prestonian Anglo-Scots were clubbed!

Marindin may have been of French origin, but he was a true-born Englishman, and I do not think that he was enamoured of Scottish professionals imported into England. He went to the dressing-room of the Albion in the old pavilion at Trent Bridge. He walked in and asked if they were all Englishmen? "Yes," was the chorused reply.

Then the Major, who was President of the F.A., remember, said: "I have very much pleasure in presenting you with the ball. You played a very good game and I hope you will win the Cup."

If a President of this era had expressed such a hope I feel that he would not have dared to take charge of the Final tie, but Marindin did; and the Albion did not win, as this was the year of the first victory of Aston Villa, who were not quite free from Scottish blood. Everyone trusted Marindin, who officiated in eight Finals. He regarded it as his duty until he resigned the Presidency. Marindin was not an ornamental President. In every sphere he was a practical man.

Lord Kinnaird succeeded to his title in 1887, but even if he was then 40 years old, he did not give up playing football for another five years. He could never understand the player who said that an extra match in mid-week was too great a strain. I heard him say on a historic occasion that he thought nothing of three hard matches a week, and then took a little exercise, in some other form, just to keep himself fit.

"Second to none," was the estimate of his ability, whether he played forward, back, or even in goal. "Any position with any club," was almost his motto. Football was the passion of his active and muscular life, and he never flinched. He played against Blackburn Rovers and their neighbours Blackburn Olympic in the early 'eighties. Yet in 1906 he wrote a letter in which he said: "I carry their marks to this day."

Between 1873 and 1883 he appeared in nine Final ties for the Cup. He was on the winning side five times—three for the Wanderers, the "celebrated Wanderers," as Major Marindin used to describe them, and twice for the Old Etonians.

Then, he was the Hon. Arthur Kinnaird. A Final was not considered complete without Arthur Kinnaird's trousers. He wore white flannel trousers, whatever jersey was necessary, and a blue and white quartered cricket cap. He had a beard of auburn hue, that some folks might have called either "ginger" or red. All this is a matter of taste, but fancy to-day meeting an opponent with a little cap surmounting a bearded face, with square powerful shoulders and "white ducks!"

At least he was resolute and robust. Major Marindin was once talking to Lord Kinnaird's mother, who regretted that "Arthur" was always playing football. She felt sure that one day he would be brought home with a broken leg. "Pray do not be alarmed," said Marindin, "for if anybody's leg is broken it will not be Arthur's."

When Charles Alcock was about, he used to tell how in a game between the Old Etonians and the Old Harrovians Kinnaird's feet were often rattling his shins. Thus provoked, Alcock stopped and said, "Are we playing hacking, Arthur?" "Oh, yes, let's have hacking," was Kinnaird's reply. "It's quite all right, now I know," added Alcock. And the pleasant game continued.

Tom Maley, of Glasgow, was once playing at Kennington Oval for a Scottish eleven against a team that included Kinnaird. "All-of-a-sudden Tom" was seen to be talking rather excitedly to Kinnaird. Said he, "If you do that again, my man, I'll pull your whiskers for ye!" A comrade, rushing up, said to Maley, "Wheest, Tam. Dae ye no ken that's the Honourable Arthur Kinnaird." But "All-of-a-sudden Tom" had not yet cooled his head and heels, for he answered, "I dinna' care wha he is. If he does that again I'll pull his whiskers."

Is it any wonder that there were ancients who used to say that Kmnnaird would not have been allowed to stay on the field five minutes in these latter days? A Scottish forward of Queen's Park was once chided for a feeble display against a certain back and he excused himself by saying, "Yon's no a man at all. He's a steam engine." He was. And Kinnaird was a similar machine, but under better control.

Yet I feel sure there was no intention to maim or hurt. Naturally, he was robust. In a letter Lord Kinnaird declared that "some of the roughest games in which I have taken part have not been with Northern or professional teams but in matches with clubs representing public schools and universities." Exactly, but these are just hard and vigorous without any mean or unfair play. As Lord Kinnaird played for over 30 years and adapted himself to all the changes of styles and alterations in the rules, he would surely have conformed to modern usages and laws.

And don't forget that Arthur Kinnaird entered Eton at the Michaelmas term of 1861. When his football education began, what did anyone know about laws of the game? Every school and college made its own laws and produced a higgledy-piggledy worse than a mixture of haggis and sauerkraut. At any rate, he played for Scotland against England and did more to popularize "Soccer" than any man who ever lived.

In all sincerity the F.A. were fortunate to have such a man on their side when the spectacular Association game was always being denounced. He was the President of the Y.M.C.A. of England and Lord High Commissioner to the Church of Scotland. He came of godly parents, who were practical in their piety. Not for me is the duty of assessing the value of his love of football.

He was staunch and unwavering, and said, "I believe that all right-minded people have good reason to thank God for the great progress of this popular national game." Kinnaird recognized that life is an education in ever-changing values and that the views and opinions of 1860 were as entirely different from those of 1900 as are those of 1914 from 1934.

Marindin was a soldier, Kinnaird a banker, and they have been followed by Clegg, who is a solicitor. Sir Charles Clegg, as he is known to this generation, is one of the three members of the Council who joined the old committee, as it was then called, before I was chosen to represent Middlesex in 1891. Mr. Clegg was elected in 1886 by the Sheffield and Hallamshire F.A. to represent them on the parent body. His first journey to London was made in the cause of amateurism. To this cause he has remained faithful throughout his long life.

Three years after joining the F.A. he was made a vice-president and when Major Marindin withdrew in 1890 he was elected Chairman of our Council, and still holds that position in conjunction with the exalted rank of President. Let me give the reader a sketch of Sir Charles, who has not always been understood and appreciated by the general public, simply because he has never courted publicity.

He has a natural reserve and is a man of few words, seldom writing long letters or making long speeches. He makes his points and avoids six words if three suffice.

Coming of a family of total abstainers from alcohol in any form, he has always been a rigid teetotaler, a determined opponent of every form of gambling, a firm upholder of pure amateurism, and a man of high principles. Having sifted out the truth of any matter, he acts upon the principle that he conceives to be just. The truth and the principle found, the details are of no consequence.

As a professional man, a lawyer, he has filled several important public positions in Sheffield; has dispensed justice as a magistrate, has been an arbitrator in trade disputes and an Official Receiver in bankruptcy.

Is it any wonder that he has applied his standard of life to the game that has always been his passion? He played football for the love of the game and he has done his utmost to govern football for the sake of the game; for its honesty, for its advancement, and for the good of all football, amateur and professional. His days have been spent in an endeavour to keep all football free from abuses, and everything it ought to be.

His powerful personality has pervaded the Council and commanded the respect of the members. A coarse tale was never told in his presence, and every man minded his speech and his step when "Charlie" Clegg was about. Not that he was lacking in wit and homely humour. He had his enjoyments. In early life he was about the best amateur runner in England from 100 yards to the quarter mile, or even the middle distance of 600 yards. As a footballer he was described in his day as "one of the fastest forwards who ever kicked a ball," and was an unerring shot at goal.

He played in the first match between England and Scotland, but he has been known to say that he did not enjoy the game. His recollections are that the great majority of the players were snobs from the South who had no use for a lawyer from Sheffield. The ball was never passed to him and nobody ever spoke to him. Mr. Clegg neither spoke to them nor desired their company. They did not understand him and he resented their air of superiority. The match over, he felt that he never wished to play in another international contest.

Of course, Sir Charles has always travelled along the broad but straight highway. He can smile. I have seen him do it when he quietly remarks, "Nobody ever gets lost on a straight road." There is a lot of meaning behind this.

When some football case or commission proves a really thorny problem, he thinks deeply. He used to speak of a man driving along the road, who pulled up and asked a walker the best way to, let us say, Wath-on-Dearne. The wayfarer, pointing to the spot where the highway forked, said, "Both will tak' thee to Wath, but whichever thee takes tha' wilt wish that tha' had takken t'other." And then Charlie Clegg would chuckle.

Another example of his relish of the plain speech of plain folk is his story of the two Sheffield grinders, who met one morning on their way to work. Tom, greeting Bill, asked "Hast tha' heeard news?" Bill: "What news?" Tom: "Why, ow'd Dick is deead." Bill: "What, ow'd Dick of Quinley's forge?" Tom: "Aye." Bill: "Well, he couldn'na' tak his brass wi' him." Tom: "No, and it would ha' melted if he had." As I have said, Clegg was misunderstood.

When all the bother broke out about the relations of the F.A. to amateurism in 1907 and *Punch* published a slashing satirical article about him, entitled "The Cleggislator," a gentleman, who must remain unknown, wrote to the Editor and told him the virtues of the head of our Association. Mr. Clegg was no longer considered a subject for ridicule or attack in any way.

Mr. Clegg never complained, but he seemed to expect that people of every rank should know his idiosyncrasies. During the war he went by arrangement to see the Secretary of State at the War Office. When Mr. Clegg entered the room he was invited to a chair and proffered a cigarette-case. As he might easily have been a member of the Anti-Tobacco League, the weed was not taken. Afterwards he remarked, "The Secretary had never taken the trouble to find out anything about the man who was coming to see him." As the Yorkshireman said, "There's now't so queer as folk."

Men are generally strange mixtures. I once heard of a sincere and devout Primitive Methodist being the chairman of a League club in the First Division. Of course, there is really no reason why he should not be. Nevertheless, the mixture of Methodism and professionalism in sport must shock the purists of amateurism.

Yet we have seen three champions of amateurism like Marindin, Kinnaird, and Clegg, all men of exemplary life and identified with the aristocracy, and imbued with missionary zeal and enthusiasm for different kinds of self-control and abstinence, taking up quite voluntarily the arduous work of governing a national sport with a big professional side.

Why did they? Because they believed that genuine amateurs should govern and rule the professional side of any game. The professional, if left to himself, runs riot and his game kills itself.

About 1907 Mr. Clegg resigned the chairmanship of the Council, owing to an acute difference in outlook. Practically the whole of the Council drew up a requisition imploring him to re-consider his decision. He came back. There was a member who refused to sign the requisition, as a protest against Clegg's autocratic ruling and general policy of supremacy. I suppose this councillor did not admire a great, strong leader.

CHAPTER IV

THE MEN FROM LANCASHIRE

ALTHOUGH the Football Association was founded by a few Southerners and the idea of the Football League was introduced by a canny Scot, who lived in Birmingham and loved "the Villa," the North country has been a great force in the development of the national winter sport. Sir Charles Clegg's work and influence have been powerful. Throughout a long life he has sacrificed himself for the sake of a game that cast a spell over the industrious toilers in the mills and mines of the North.

The game was captured from the classes, and the masses had a different point of view. The leader from Yorkshire saw that football was an inheritance for every man. And there were men in Lancashire with as broad an outlook.

Surely, too, this was the outlook of the Old Etonians, for when the gentlemen who had been at this great school first played in an Association Cup tie, against Darwen in February, 1879, and the Eton aristocrats won after two drawn games, it is interesting to recall that £175 was raised by subscriptions to enable the Lancashire lads, the cotton operatives, to have what is now called special training. Of this amount £10 was contributed by the Football Association, and £5 by the Old Etonians. Let me ask you, can you imagine a crack professional club in these days giving any money to a Third Division team so that they could train by the seaside for the coming struggle between them?

Yet, in a way, that has been the spirit of Clegg, the stern sportsman. In other forms that was also the spirit of Lancashire in the long ago, save that they wanted to help themselves and not depend upon other folks. They did not want to be the recipients of aid from their opponents, however praiseworthy might be their sportsmanship.

Lancashire had their own ideas. Recall the old saying, "What Lancashire thinks to-day England thinks to-morrow." The Lancashire clubs in the early 'eighties saw that this was the people's game, and crowds were rushing to the matches. They decided that the players who attracted spectators should be paid for their skill. As we all know, this was done secretly at first. After a few years the secrecy was no longer necessary, for professionalism was sanctioned and payments were made over the club table and not under it.

Lancashire, through Preston North End, brought professional football into the world, and ever since there have been problems of control for the Association, and much ingenuity to enable all clubs to pay their way. The Football Association have not been so much concerned with their solvency as with their honesty as demanded by the regulations and laws of the game.

Lancashire projected the formation of a British Football Association as a rival to the F.A., but nothing came of it.

When I became Secretary to the F.A. there were five men from Lancashire on the Council. They were Dr. Morley, of Blackburn Rovers, the senior vice-president, Messrs. J.J. Bentley (Bolton Wanderers), D.B. Woolfall (Accrington), R.P. Gregson (Lancashire Association), and R.B. Lythgoe (Liverpool). And one of the auditors was Mr. Tom Hindle, of Darwen, the other being Mr. J. Campbell Orr (Birmingham). All of them have passed away.

In his day Edward S. Morley, M.D., was very well known and what some people would call a "character." He was the brother of the Rt. Hon. John Morley, who became Lord Morley, was a doctor practising in Blackburn and had been the chairman of the Rovers. A great lover of the game, he was a familiar figure with his top hat, his velvet coat and his cigar. Indeed, the cigar was as much a part of Dr. Morley as of the late Lord Birkenhead.

A well-meaning friend once introduced Dr. Morley as "the brother of the Right Honourable John, you know." The little doctor flared up and rasped out, "Not so much of your d——d reflected glory, please." He was quite content to stand alone, top-hat and all that. He remained a director of the Rovers until he died, and his slogan on the stand or anywhere else was, "For Heaven's sake, Rovers, play *football*."

His enthusiasm may be accounted for by a remark he once made: "I am determined to keep my heart young. Football provides me with the only bit of relaxation I allow myself amid the cares and monotony of everyday life, and I will not willingly let it go." To me that seems to express simply the feelings of millions of people the world over.

The doctor did not like the idea of men being paid for playing the game when it was first mooted, but when the vote was taken at the meeting called by the Football Association, Dr. Morley proposed that the report of the Committee to the effect that it was "expedient to legalize the employment of professionals under restriction," be adopted. That was carried by an overwhelming majority in July, 1885. He never recanted.

There was a strong element of pugnacity in his equipment. Some time before I became a member of the Council, Dr. Morley made his first appearance before this body in connection with a dispute between Blackburn Rovers and Darwen. He was accompanied by Mr. John Lewis, at that time the honorary secretary of the Rovers. Dr. Morley astounded the F.A. by his opening remark: "We have come, to meet your wishes, but you have no authority to ask us to do so and you have no right to enter into the disagreement between ourselves and Darwen." Although this was not quite the way to induce a sympathetic reception, the doctor's facts and logic won the day.

When I got to know Dr. Morley well, I liked his frankness and combative temper. Within eighteen months of my becoming Secretary to the F.A., Dr. Morley wrote me a letter in which he remarked, "I understand that a certain person on the Council is giving you trouble. Why don't you tell him to go to the Devil? I should."

The Football Association gave Blackburn Rovers a shield to commemorate their three consecutive victories in the Final ties of

1883-4-5 and asked the loan of it for an exhibition of some kind—
I forget exactly what—at the Crystal Palace in 1897. Dr. Morley
wrote me saying, "I have instructed the Rovers' Secretary to call
at my house for the shield, which he will send direct to the Crystal
Palace. The shield is mine, and I trust that Providence may not take
it into His head to call me hence before the close of the Exhibition,
as were this to happen the shield would be wanted as furniture for
my coffin. I don't think you have seen the monstrosity, but I assure
you it is fit for nothing but garnishing a coffin lid and to this use I
have dedicated it."

Yes, this was the combative gentleman who in another letter
described a proposition by Mr. N.L. Jackson as impertinent. He
expressed himself thus: "Even if Lord Kinnaird is present I mean to
have a fair innings re Jackson, and I am looking forward to a very
enjoyable time. I do like a fight if anybody will take the trouble to
tread on the tail of my coat."

Just before Christmas in the Diamond Jubilee year he had
heard of a meeting to consider the conditions for a cup or shield to
be given by a well-known firm of whisky distillers, and discussing
the proposal he wrote: "I should like to suggest as a coat-of-
arms for this cup— a keg of whisky, with a gibbet on each side as
supports; a man and woman hanging on either side."

Perhaps this faculty of outspokenness was inherited by the
doctor's son, who was reputed to be the author of a forcible
article, in the old "Pall Mall Gazette," upon the people who came
to London to see a Final tie at Kennington Oval in the Victorian
era. He described the invasion as being made by the "Northern
hordes." At least this may be said, that in Blackburn he was spoken
of as the author.

How times have changed! For nowadays, "all the world and
his wife" come to our spring festival at Wembley, and the London
newspapers regard the occasion as a manifestation of national
interest in one of the thrilling events of the year, just as much as
the Derby.

There were two other men from Blackburn on our Council
when I took office. Mr. Dan Woolfall, who was at one time

connected with Blackburn Rovers, succeeded the late Mr. C.E. Hart as our honorary treasurer in 1901, and from 1906 to 1914, he was President of the Fédération Internationale de Football Association. During that period England was considered the paramount power in football on the Continent, and Woolfall was held in high esteem for his judgment and impartiality. He gave a lot of his time to the game and to the affairs of the F.A., for he was an able administrator and had a keen eye for any financial malpractice. As he was a highly-placed civil servant concerned with the income-tax department of the Inland Revenue, he knew, perhaps, something of how clever some persons can be over money. But he was a man that Clegg appreciated.

The other man from Blackburn was Mr. R.P. Gregson, known to his intimates as "Dick." Now, he was an artistic photographer, and as a member of the International Selection Committee he attended all the big matches and took group pictures of our team. He was by way of being scientific in mind and I shall never forget how he worked among the dying and the seriously injured on the dreadful day of the Ibrox disaster in 1902. For hours he was in his shirt sleeves, tireless—ambulance men had not then commenced to attend great football matches. If I may say so, and not be misunderstood, he was in his element.

A sound judge of a footballer, his criticisms were often tinged with wit. As time after time he saw a player shoot above the cross-bar, he would say that if every footballer who failed in this way, when well placed to score, was fined threepence, the National Debt would soon be wiped out! That was before the European War. Nowadays such a joke could not be appreciated.

Gregson was a valuable member of the Council and not too talkative. Perhaps the most helpful plan he was the means of inventing and introducing was the scheme of exemptions in relation to the Association Cup ties. As soon as the League system of matches was devised, and the dates of fixtures were definite and unchangeable without permission of the League, such a change was needed. Gregson foresaw that professionalism, of which he became a champion as soon as he was convinced that to try and stop the new development was as futile as the effort of Canute when he had a seaside holiday and discovered the limitations of royalty, demanded consideration and concessions. Therefore he invented the Qualifying Competition for the Association Cup with a number of exemptions. But he did not take all the credit to himself, for he insisted that the Town Clerk of Blackburn, Mr. W.E.L. Game, had as much to do with the scheme as himself. His knowledge of the game was peculiar and intimate.

John Bentley, the journalist, devoted his life, boy and man, to football. He will probably be best remembered as the solid man who was the defender in the Council Chamber of the League transfer system. All the talk about the "buying and selling of players" being unsportsmanlike left him quite unmoved. A hard-headed practical person, he felt that this plan protected the weaker clubs, stifled poaching and all its cunning approaches, created a working basis for clubs, raised the status of the player, advanced his wages, insured him summer pay and gave both club and player a feeling of permanence—most important when there are staffs of professional players.

Many people, myself included, still feel that there are aspects of the transfer system that might be amended in the interests of the player, but these are matters that do not trouble the public as a whole. Bentley was undoubtedly a friend to players and had a great respect for professionals, most of whom he rightly regarded as thoroughly decent fellows. He used to tell the story that one day he was out walking with a company of ladies and gentlemen. They met several young men, well dressed and groomed, who raised their hats. "Who are they?" came the question, and Bentley answered, "Only those disreputable football professionals you sometimes talk about." He could be very relentless with his dry wit.

This later generation have little knowledge of Bob Lythgoe, for so long the master-mind of the Liverpool Association, an organization that he created. I never asked him, but I thought he was a Welshman. Not a bit of one, for he was born at Warrington. Perchance the reader may wonder where that is—he had better ask George Duckworth, the Lancashire wicket-keeper. The idea that he was Welsh arose from the fact that early in life he was goalkeeper to the Druids, who, of course, are identified with Ruabon, part of a district that used to produce players as naturally as the daisies spring up in the fields.

A thin man of medium height, is it any wonder that Lythgoe soon gave up the job of guarding the entrance to the goal? In his day the Goalkeepers' Protection Act had not been passed by the International Board, and the keeper had to look after himself.

As I have been a bit of a goalkeeper myself, I know. Somebody must have thought that "young Wall" could stop a shot or he would never have kept goal for the London Football Association. In my time, the custodian had to keep one eye on the ball and the other eye on some merciless forward who would charge him or heave him a yard or two, while one of his mates placed the ball between the posts and under the tape. The keeper felt that every man's hand in the enemy camp was against him.

And let me remind the reader that there were no goal-nets then. Many a goal was awarded when the ball had never passed between the posts. I have heard that John Bentley was once refereeing a match—I am not sure, but if I remember rightly it was an international game—when a goal was claimed. The linesmen, or the umpires as they were then called, agreed that the ball had flashed between the posts, and in those days if the linesmen agreed, the referee was not called upon to give a decision. Therefore a goal was counted, but Bentley knew that this was not the case. He learned afterwards from the players that a goal had not been scored.

From this one example the necessity and value of the goal-net is obvious. A former Rugby player, Mr. J.A. Brodie, the city engineer of Liverpool, was the inventor of the netting arrangement with which everybody is now familiar. After he had thought out the idea, which he felt recommended itself, Mr. Brodie saw Bob Lythgoe and had a chat with him about goals. In twenty minutes Mr. Brodie settled the actual design in his mind. He got the nets made and, being a busy city official, put them aside altogether for twelve months.

Then someone in a football periodical said that a goal-net would be a good thing. Mr. Brodie wrote to the Editor and said that he had got some made. Mr. Bentley asked Mr. Brodie if he would put the nets up on the Bolton Wanderers' ground, for their match with Nottingham Forest. Mr. Brodie had tried them before on the Old Etonian ground, now the Anfield entrance of the Liverpool club. They were first used on Everton's old ground, then given a trial with a single net for one goal in a match at Bolton, and finally and officially introduced in a North and South trial match at Nottingham in 1891. The nets were an instantaneous success, and were soon in general use by order.

I remember a newspaper asking how many lives these nets had saved? Of course, the question related to referees. The funny part of the story is that a famous international Soccer player made this remark to Bob Lythgoe: "Why the blazes is Brodie bothering his head about these nets for goals? He knows something about the Rugby game, but not about our kind of football." But he did. I was told over twenty years ago that this same Mr. Brodie became the adviser to the Indian Government on the lay-out of Delhi, when it was made the new capital of the Dependency. The Corporation of the City of Liverpool gave him leave of absence.

Thus you see that after all Lancashire has done much for our game, by working hard for the introduction of open professionalism, by devising the exemption system for Cup ties, and by fashioning nets designed to obviate mistakes or misconceptions about goals. This county has sent many valuable men to our Council and provided England with so many fine players that it would be an insuperable task to grade them. That, however, is another story.

CHAPTER V

FORTY YEARS BACK—TWO GREAT FORWARDS

THE most tremendous change in the Association football of my time does not concern the professional phase of the game. The professionals, ten years after Dr. Morley carried his resolution in favour of the recognition of the status of the paid player, included many of the best we have ever been able to call upon to represent England. But at that time the amateurs from the public schools, and the varsities, and members of the Corinthians were almost as clever. The only differences I can recall were that the amateurs were not so adroit in heading the ball, and not, as a rule, in such fine physical condition.

What do we see in these days? The professionals in League teams have changed their style, due, in my opinion, to the stress of competition and to the alteration in the law relating to off-side. Incidentally, let me say here that the change of the off-side law was only partly due to the continual stoppages caused by backs who anticipated the pass, the next move, and by taking up a more advanced position caused the man who received the ball to be off-side—which really means off his side for the moment; for the fraction of a second he was out of the game.

This trick of stopping the play for a free-kick, relieving the defence, was not so easy as it looked. There was, indeed, a very exact calculation of time by the back and his mates. Not only so, but it was very often a "nice point" for referees to decide. Over and over again during this era of a move that reminded many of the art of chess, I heard Sir Charles Clegg say that the law would have to be changed. He would declare that "we shall have to make the game easier for the forwards."

I have an idea that he was right, but I have always felt that the professional teams have not, as a whole, taken full advantage of the greater scope given to forwards, because of the fantastic formations they have introduced into their games. However, we will let that pass, if I may adapt the words of Jack Point, and return to our story.

Now, the amateurs of these latter days are not nearly up to the standard of the professional. There are more amateurs than ever, and they can show us good football. The average is better than in 1895, the year that I am writing about, but the very best are not equal to the best of forty years ago.

Generally, the introduction of professionalism is blamed for this decline, but it may more truly be said that many of the old Public Schools have given up playing our game because the headmaster and the university men who are taking their salary as gamesmasters, have a prejudice against professionalism in this particular sport. That which is accepted in most games cannot be tolerated in Association football. The "facts" in support of this attitude can be left in abeyance. The cause of the rarity of first-class amateurs is quite another story.

When England played Ireland at Derby in 1895, a wholly professional eleven won by 9–1. Within ten days, England met Wales, one goal each being the result. The English eleven, entirely amateurs, consisted of members of the Corinthian club, just the same as in 1894. In this latter year the English-Corinthian team won by 5–1, but in 1895 each side scored once. Now mark what happened. When England faced Scotland on Everton's new ground, two only of these Corinthians were again chosen.

L.V. Lodge, of Cambridge University, retained his position as a back and R.C. Gosling, of the Old Etonians, was made the captain and moved from inside-right to inside-left. This was a judicious move, for Bloomer, who had scored two goals in his first international match, that against Ireland in the previous month (March), was again the inside man to Billy Bassett on the right, while the left wing was entirely new, Gosling being partner to

Steve Smith, the outside-left who was then such a success with Aston Villa. And the Scottish team was beaten by 3–0, Bloomer beginning his series of goals against Scotland and Steve Smith getting the second.

The half-back line was of little men—John Reynolds, of Aston Villa, an Irishman in 1891, but a true-born Englishman in 1892 (think that over); John Holt, the Everton Jack-in-the-Box, a regular spring-heel Jack in rising for the ball and tackling his enemy unawares, so to speak; and Ernest Needham, of Sheffield United, the sturdy sobersides who stole the ball and made another chum the receiver. How great were these three little men, the tallest not more than 5 ft. 5 in., which also was about the height of Steve Smith, of Hednesford.

Just fancy Robert Cunliffe Gosling, to give his name in full, in front of Needham and by the side of Smith. It brings to mind the joke that Will Crooks made more than once when in aristocratic company. He used to say: "Fancy me on the same platform as Lord Cecil"—or some other peer.

Yes, there was Cunliffe Gosling, the immaculate Old Etonian, looking every inch the high-born (no joke intended), for he was well over six feet, and thirteen stone in weight—bone and muscle, not the soft flesh that some amateurs took into the English eleven against Scotland in 0000—the date does not matter. England's trainer complained that their flesh was as soft as that of women—before they began to act as men.

Gosling's carriage and gait would have done credit to a court chamberlain at a levee, but his play was superb—all polish and perfection. As unselfish as anybody I ever saw on the field. There were times when he might have held the ball rather than tap it to a comrade not nearly so sure in shooting and so clever in control. His play was the very refinement of football, and mind, effective football.

He looked the gentleman he was, suave, kindly and never unfair. But let anybody tackle him and try to nudge him off the ball! After impact with his massive proportions, with the impetus of a fleet runner, the tackler knew what a charge meant. He would be inclined to shake himself like a dog, with the air of assuring himself that all his limbs were still attached and functioning.

Many of those amateurs of thirty and forty years ago were more like the modern Rugby forward than anyone I can compare them with. There are an extraordinary number of little men in Association football to-day. Still, as one of them once said to me: "We are nearer to our work on the ground than these scarlet runners." There were many of those amateurs, so formidable in build that I can never forget them.

I don't know, but I have often wondered, whether Cunliffe Gosling was the richest man who ever played for England by the side of a professional. I cannot say, but his will was proved at over £700,000.

The other amateur, L.V. Lodge, was playing for Cambridge University at the same time that C.B. Fry, W.J. Oakley and G.O. Smith were in the football elevens of the Dark Blues. Lodge, who came from Durham School, also played bandy, a kind of hockey, but whatever he played he was a back, a position for which nature had fitted him.

Strong and long-legged, he was red-haired and had all the dash and fire that this colour is supposed to signify. A splendid tackler of the dashing, fearless sort, he was also a sure kicker of a ball. Although he was partnered by James Crabtree, one of the soundest and most versatile players that Aston Villa ever had, he did not suffer by comparison as a back in this match. As John W. Sutcliffe, the Rugby back who became the goalkeeper of Bolton Wanderers, was behind this pair, it is not astonishing that Scotland never scored.

About twenty-one years after the match Lodge, who had been missing, was found drowned at Buxton. Such a close to his life was quite irreconcilable with his characteristics as a footballer. I wonder whether either Gosling or Lodge was any the worse for their experience with these professional footballers, or footpads as they were clubbed by some of the critics of 1895.

Among the survivors of this team who so handsomely defeated the Scots there is another "Steve," a christian name as much associated with Bloomer as with Donoghue in silk and saddle. There is a story told that when Bloomer was first proposed as inside-right for the match against Ireland, about a month before he faced Scotland, a member of the International Selection Committee, our dear departed friend Charles Crump, asked: "Who is Bloomer?" Whether the story can be proved true I doubt, but there was no necessity to inquire again, for he was the free gift of Nature to football. I have seen multitudes of players, but never a more effective inside-forward in a big match.

The greater the match the better he played. This is the decisive test of a man in any sport; the capacity to rise above his normal form, to give his best when the best is needed. As he is still with us and occasionally watches a match, such as England v. Austria and a tense Cup tie, it is evident that the passing of years has not killed his interest in the game.

He and John Goodall went to see the tie between Arsenal and Derby County, his old club with which his name will always be linked, in February, 1934. How he must have longed to be young enough to have played!

When 46 years of age, in 1920, he was careful to point out that the place of his birth was Cradley Heath, which is in Worcestershire, and not in Staffordshire. His parents moved to Derby when he was five years old. He learned his football with the Derby Swifts, a club of school boys. John Goodall, who happened to be born in London, but was brought up in Kilmarnock and became a player of the Scottish type, before he joined Great Lever and then Preston North End in its famous days, was with Derby County and saw the boy Bloomer when he was one of the Swifts.

Various people have claimed the credit of discovering Bloomer, but Goodall is entitled to it from what I heard one day, when England were playing Scotland at the Crystal Palace. If I remember rightly this was Bloomer's twenty-first appearance in England's national eleven. Bloomer said that day that "Goodall took the greatest interest in me when I was a kid. He coached me, secured me for Derby County, played with me and never failed to give me valuable hints and advice." Yes, he was engaged for 7s. 6d.

per week!

In 1893 on the Victoria Grounds, Stoke, Bloomer made his first appearance at inside-right in a League match against the chief club of the Potteries. There was a vacancy and Goodall, the captain of Derby County, recommended him at 19 years of age for the position. He finished his career on January 24, 1914, when 40 years old. His club had the confidence to ask him at that age to play centre-forward against Bradford City, and he had the courage to do so.

Of course, he scored hundreds of goals. The football annuals tell us that his total in League games was just over 350, but he once reckoned them to be 450. I am not a keeper of statistics, but I do know that he was a match-winner and got 28 goals for England; eight against Scotland, eleven against Ireland and nine against Wales. His first against Scotland was in 1895, and his last in 1907.

Some of the newspapers used to say that Bloomer got his usual goal. Once it was reported that Bloomer got his goal, but that was all he did! One smiled, for a goal covers a multitude of sins on the field.

Yes, he was a great marksman, and his splendid passes were generally made with one touch. He had no time for fancy work. Bloomer, of course, made mistakes like everyone else, but he was the superior of everyone I ever saw as a scorer. A great volleyer in front of goal, he placed his ground shots at a fast pace, out of the reach of the keeper and slantwise. But the keepers used to say that it was difficult to tell which foot he would use for a shot. They have been known to say, "Steve, you would not have beaten me this time but you changed your foot."

And he had an intense admiration for G.O. Smith. The Old Carthusian, according to both Goodall and Bloomer, was so easy to play with, and he was a man without petty pride. Smith used to call out "Steve," and he made the position so favourable that in the twinkling of an eye the ball was in the net. And whether you counted it a good shot or not, Bloomer held that there was never a bad shot that scored. I firmly believe that Bloomer in many respects never had a superior.

Just as one felt at a glance that Gosling was an aristocrat, so one realized that Bloomer was a son of the people—born, as Goodall said, with a football at his toe. He had an erect and finely proportioned figure and his movements were always balanced.

His pale face was a mystery to me. Some thought that his pallor was due to physical weakness, but this was an idea that his vitality and endurance, maintained for years, abundantly disproved. I often thought when I watched him in big matches that this sickly cast of countenance was caused by anxiety and the way he taxed his nervous energy, for he was often deadly serious. He seldom played for Derby County as he did for England.

Some of the men chosen for England in these latter days have not his intense desire to win. And it is a pointed commentary on the luck, or the misfortune, of a football career that such a forward, ranked amongst the best of any era, failed to realize his greatest ambition—the gold medal given to the winners of the Association Cup.

I dare say you have heard the story of the new half-back who was anxious to make a name and went up to James Ross in his days with Manchester City. He asked him to point out Ross. Ross intimated that the particular gentleman he was in quest of was "that fair-haired fellow over there." The player he pointed out was Sammy Frost, the Millwall man who went North.

Frost withstood the attention he received for a time until, lying in the mud, he looked up and put the question: "What's the gime, mate?" "Oh," said the new and ambitious recruit, "you're a darned Cockney! I thought you were a Scottie. I've got mixed."

Bloomer used to tell a very similar tale, about a player in South Wales wishing to know "which was Bloomer." That day, owing to mishaps among the team on tour, the Derby crack was at outside-left, and he referred the inquirer to his substitute at inside-right. I suppose these experiences are called practical jokes; very practical indeed for Frost and the man who personated Bloomer.

It really does not matter whether Bloomer scored 350 or 450 goals. The point that occurs to me is that he stands out as the greatest goal-getter in first-class football. His success was due to constant shooting. He tried to take every chance, every half-chance, from any angle, that presented itself. There was no hesitation about him, seldom a desire to trap the ball or steady it, rarely a wish to pass to a comrade unless he was better placed than himself, and never the least intention of re-transferring the ball to the wing-raiders.

Apply these remarks to what is often seen in class matches of to-day, and it will be clear why more goals are not scored. Many forwards do not shoulder the responsibility of shooting. Anybody can have the ball, expresses their attitude.

Bloomer wanted the ball near goal, and men like G.O. Smith and Goodall saw that he received it. All three of them were footballers. Bloomer lived to shoot, to pick up stray balls that rebounded off a back or were diverted towards him accidentally. Then he crashed the ball into the net.

Scottish backs knew his searching glance, always on the look-out for the ball. One might almost say that all Scotland thanked the Lord when Bloomer ceased to play.

When he returned to England after a long absence abroad, either after being a prisoner at Ruhleben during the war, or when he went out to coach troops in Canada, he was asked what he thought of English games? He replied that the forwards did not shoot often enough. After all my honest praise of Bloomer, we ought not to forget that there is a lesson to be learned from his brilliant career. This can be condensed into, "Shoot, brothers, shoot," a parody of a line I sang at school, in the Canadian Boat Song.

Some forwards, ancient and modern, have practised shooting. One of the old school used to place a pole in the middle of the goal and shoot to the right and left of it with either foot. And he was a Scotsman and deserved to be the good player he was.

CHAPTER VI

OTHER BRILLIANT PLAYERS OF THE PAST

THE spread of Association football all over the world is the greatest tribute to this British game. Even in the days when the pastime was crude the players must have felt that the rough and tumble was a mirror of life with its ups and downs, its successes and failures, its revels and risks.

And all the laws, rules and refinements that have been introduced have not been able to diminish its appeal to all races, to people of every colour, and to men of every creed. There is human nature in football. Britons have taken this manly sport wherever they have travelled.

After one of Shackleton's voyages to the Antarctic a lecture was given in the Queen's Hall, London, by one of his officers. Photographs were thrown upon a screen and we saw the crew playing the game as well as they could on the ice. Of all the pictures exhibited, none evoked so much appreciation and applause from a fashionable gathering as the snapshot of this match. And this by an assembly that could never have been suspected of having the slightest interest in the people's game.

The Football Association have spared no effort to encourage and develop the playing of the game. The first official team sent over the English Channel went to Berlin in 1899. I did not go, but when the players returned, no tale caused so much merriment as the experience of William Bassett on the Tempelhofer Field. A half-back was told never to leave Herr Bassett, to be with him wherever he went. "Herr" Bassett soon discovered these instructions, and just to see if he was right, he went off the playing area, ran behind one of the goals and re-entered the arena on the other side of the net. The half-back went with him and never left him. Naturally Bassett, now the chairman of West Bromwich Albion, laughed and led his close companion many a merry dance.

The house of Hohenzollern saw that football was an admirable form of body culture. Some of the young princes played the game, which was taken up with the thoroughness that is characteristic of the German. That is merely one example.

In November, 1906, an amateur eleven visited Paris and won by teens of goals. With the help of the clubs, teams were sent all over the Continent, and in many countries English coaches were employed. This missionary work has had many sequels.

The first was the desire of the South African Association that we should send a team to tour their country. That was in 1910. Such a journey, with matches arranged at various centres from Cape Town to Pretoria, from Port Elizabeth to Kimberley, was a big undertaking. Our clubs were not easily persuaded to release the players who wanted to make the trip. Eventually we were promised the help of talented players, who were entertained to dinner the night before they embarked.

I have never kept a diary, but I remember that some members of the International Selection Committee and guests sat in the lounge of the hotel after the players had gone to bed. We were all anxious about the illness of King Edward VII, and just before midnight we learned by telephone that His Majesty had passed away. The announcement was depressing, but the team quietly left London next morning with Mr. Charles J. Hughes, one of our vice-presidents, as the honorary conductor.

Throughout his life Mr. Hughes had been devoted to the sport, as an amateur player and as a referee without price, for he never took a fee; and as a member of the Council he had been in charge of most of the elevens who visited the Continent.

"Charlie" Hughes was what we call nowadays a good "mixer," and not a one-sport man. His sympathies were broad. He was liked by all who knew him, and it was with the unanimous wish of the council that he undertook the honorary position of the man-in-charge of the first representative teams that the F.A. sent to parts of the Empire—South Africa, Australia and Canada.

Mr. Hughes went alone, but it seemed to me that such an undertaking required two gentlemen as joint managers. His health was undermined and he was never quite the same man again. Since that painful experience there have always been two members of the Council chosen for these onerous duties.

There were five amateurs in the party, these including Vivian Woodward, as captain, and Arthur Berry, the Oxford University outside-right, who played for England against Ireland in 1909, appeared in the Olympic Games of 1908 in London and of 1912 at Stockholm, when the United Kingdom won on each occasion. Apart from these events Berry was awarded about 20 caps for international matches confined to amateurs.

A thorough amateur, he was a bonny player—very clever and fairly fast. He helped Liverpool, Everton, Fulham, Wrexham and other clubs.

It is quite possible that Berry is not known to this generation, and may not be recalled by some of their elders, but Woodward and Berry formed one of the very best right-wing pairs that England ever had in their amateur elevens. That is why I have coupled them. What I am not able to understand is why neither Woodward nor Berry was ever elected a member of the Corinthians.

So far as I know, neither ever played for the Corinthians, but the Liverpool gentleman, Berry, himself the son of a solicitor, became a barrister and probably gave up the game before the war. Still, he was very prominent from 1908 to 1913, and was a familiar figure in almost every country then playing football.

Vivian Woodward's name has been known all over the world—for he has been on tour in the United States as well as South Africa, and has taken part in about 70 matches when his team has been representing England. No doubt the great majority of these have been restricted to amateurs, but his caps in the older series of international contests must run into the teens. Scotland knew all about him and rejoiced when so telling a ball player was not in England's eleven.

I am going to make a statement that may be considered startling, but as my opinion is honest, I am not concerned if it does not agree with the views of others. G.O. Smith and Woodward were both great players, but the Tottenham and Chelsea forward was the better. Why was he the better footballer? Woodward was the more versatile, the more consistent, and cleverer with his heading.

Not only was he a remarkable centre-forward, but he was at least quite as effective at either inside-right or inside-left. I believe that Woodward has stated that the Corinthians never asked him to play for them! This is astounding. I am sure that Woodward would have appreciated such an invitation as much as any that he received even from the Football Association.

Possibly, nay probably, he would have overshadowed some of the Corinthian celebrities. There are those who still think that Vivian Woodward, George Hilsdon and James Windridge were, as a set, three of the finest inside forwards who ever played together, as they did for England against Scotland, in 1908, when the match was drawn owing to the remarkable goal that Windridge scored.

Woodward, who was an architect and surveyor, was a strong-looking young man of twenty-three when he came out with Tottenham Hotspurs. Very nearly 5 ft. 11 in., he weighed at that time 11 st. I rather fear that the strenuous game he played took a lot of vitality out of him. Strenuous is used in the sense of sapping his own strength rather than in applying it outwardly to his opponents.

Force was never his motto. A man who had perfect control of the ball with either foot, he was a wonderful judge of the moment to make the pass to a chum who would foresee where Woodward would next be for the return pass. His adroitness with either the inside or outside of his foot was only equalled by the accuracy of his heading.

With the exception of Alec Turnbull ("Sandy"), of Manchester, and Dean, of Everton, in these latter days, Woodward was as dangerous near goal with his head as any man I have seen. And it should be remembered that Woodward—they called him

"Jack"—was faster than he looked, and that he had a neat trick of feinting, or what some call "selling the dummy." The most unselfish of forwards, he was a master-model of team work. He must have scored hundreds of goals.

In the 23 matches of this South African tour in 1910, he was the chief scorer with 32 goals, but there were others who distinguished themselves.

Now let me say that Woodward was soft-spoken, courteous, modest; he never talked about his football, and seldom discussed that of his mates. If he could not speak well of a man he preferred silence. He was devoted to his mother, whom he often took to matches, and did not leave her until she was comfortably seated.

In many respects he was a man who stood alone, combining unsuspected strength of mind and body with a suavity of manner. His personality and play left an abiding impression on the football of South Africa, and there have been not a few who have talked about the seed that was sown by Woodward. The boys, especially those at school, watched him closely.

The harvest was gathered some fourteen years after, in 1924, when South Africa sent a team of amateurs to England. Well they played, for our elevens, representing the strength of English amateurism, could only win the international contests at Southampton and Tottenham by 3–2. I am not so sure that the F.A. side ought to have won at Tottenham. A draw would have more justly reflected the merits of the teams.

Woodward was never a man who lived out of the game. He lived for the game, although he also played cricket. The Football Association found it difficult to get a bill of expenses from him. When the European war broke out he was one of the first to join the Football Battalion of the 17th Middlesex. He was, too, one of the first casualties, but he survived, attained the rank of major, and afterwards devoted himself to farming in Essex, a county that he knew well in his early days.

I have referred to the Scotland and England match of 1908 at Hampden Park. Woodward, Hilsdon and Windridge were our inside forwards. Does the reader remember the centre half-back?

Memory plays tricks with us. His name was William Wedlock, and he was a member of the team sent to South Africa in 1910. I am compelled to couple his name with his captain, Woodward, for they were the most arresting figures of the tour.

Wedlock was popular with everybody. He never courted popularity, but he was one of those little men, in stature only, who arouse a kindly feeling because they are little. Wedlock appealed as a player, a great centre half-back, in all but height, and let me say forthwith that he was a great natural gentleman. From Lord Methuen and his lady, who once desired that he should be presented, to plain "Mr. Brown," everyone wished to talk with Wedlock.

In this era men of the build of the Life Guards are preferred, for the club managers like them because the ball is so often in the air. Yet the records tell us about Johnny Holt who was 5 ft. 4 in., Tom Morren 5 ft. 5 in. and Wedlock 5ft. 4½ in., who all played for England and could "get up" to the ball in the air. I once heard a free-spoken man on the grandstand say that Wedlock was "a devil to climb!"

Wedlock did not look like a footballer, although many men of strange shapes and appearances have been successful. Although only 5 ft. 4½ in., Wedlock weighed 10 st. 10 lb. His shoulders were broad, and he was universally called "Fatty" in his native Bristol. The word merely meant muscle in bulk. His face had a look of repose, but the keen eye and the firm mouth indicated determination. His smile was winning, but seldom seen on the field.

When I first spoke to him I was surprised, for instead of the soft speech of Somerset and Gloucester, I heard the accent and crispness of the Welshman. He had lived in Wales and played for a Welsh club. No doubt the Welsh Association made inquiries about his birth-place. Bedminster was a place "without" their jurisdiction. Little Wedlock was always under the eye of a Bristol City director, and as a "boy-footballer" went to that club.

He soon made a name, and was chosen as reserve in a Trial Match between Amateurs and Professionals on Sheffield

Wednesday's ground. Veitch, of Newcastle, was the centre half-back selected, but he got injured and Wedlock was rushed from Bristol to Owlerton (the name of the ground since changed to Hillsborough). Arriving late, he ran on to the field, and the first thing he did was to trip up Woodward.

In the excitement caused by a hurried motor drive to the ground his mental balance must have been upset, for he was a clean honest-to-goodness player. Never again did he offend.

He filled the eye that afternoon, and for years afterwards he was the recognized centre half-back of England, and that at a time when a player so big and clever as Charles Roberts, of Manchester United, was in his prime. The merits and points of two men so dissimilar in build were always being discussed by the public, but our International Selection Committee preferred Wedlock above all men.

Even at this lapse of time most people think of Wedlock as a wonder, as the very Puck of football in any age. This is not to say that he was "a rough, knurly-limbed, faun-faced, shock-pated, mischievous little urchin," as our old friend the Bard of Avon describes Puck among the fairies.

Yet Wedlock could fill all space. He was always with the ball; its closest companion. In most matches he would play the ball thrice to the once of any other man. With either foot he was useful, but his heading was arresting. The crowd had to look at him and laugh.

People could not help laughing, for he headed the ball with automatic precision. The taller opponent rarely could beat Wedlock, who bobbed up serenely to head and to head again. Sometimes he seemed to have been constructed for heading, for he did so when he might have kicked. Yet he knew where he was putting the ball. His adversaries must have regarded him as a Paul Pry, a meddlesome, dwarfish demon always interfering and intruding to upset the plans of other folks for whom he had no sympathy.

To most onlookers he signified perpetual motion. After ten or eleven months of continuous travel and football he was chosen to play against Ireland at Derby in February, 1911, when a strong English eleven won by the odd goal of three. The prime factor in beating the Irishmen was Wedlock. Throughout the game he had the energy of a swift-flowing wide river.

Mr. C. Stewart Caine, the renowned sporting writer and critic, saw the match, and when it was over he said: "What sort of man is this Wedlock? Is he made of flesh and blood the same as other players?" The way he bounced about for a stern ninety minutes suggested that he was an indiarubber man. Could he ever become tired?

He never waited to see the effect of what he had done. The moment he had played the ball he was moving to another position; he was always thinking, his everlasting question being: What next?

If he decided to advance and shoot at goal, the ball had no sooner left his boot than he turned round and ran back to his central position. His action seemed to say: "If I score I shall hear the people cheer. I shall not do any good by standing still watching the ball. If I don't score, then the ball will be returned by a back, probably down the field. I must be there waiting for the clearance kick."

That is the sort of man he was; always thinking a move ahead of the play and about what would happen to the side. To watch his shot, to see what happened to the ball, might satisfy his own curiosity, but would be of no benefit to the team.

The most arresting feature of his play was his determination to be near the ball. It was the ball he wanted; not the man. He was everywhere, at least he seemed to be.

Now this little man, beside doing his duty for Bristol City, took part in 28 international matches between 1907 and 1912. In 1912–13 he was not available owing to injury, but he played one more match against Wales at Cardiff in the spring of 1914, when another little man, McNeal, of West Bromwich, was on his left. That makes 29 matches against Scotland, Ireland, Wales, Austria, Hungary, Bohemia and South Africa. When he sailed for Cape Town he remarked that such a tour was an education, as valuable to him as going to either Oxford or Cambridge was to a rich man.

He had the same idea about all his jaunts.

A retiring man of few words, he loved the game he played for a livelihood. His three elder brothers set him the example of playing, and, in his early days, Hugh Wilson and A. Annan, two well-known Scottish players from Sunderland, gave him valuable hints. Always grateful to them, he nevertheless was convinced that quick thinking and rapid decisions were the greatest factors in all football. That was more than ever his opinion when speed became so common. He was a most remarkable player.

CHAPTER VII

WHY AMATEURS ARE NOT CHOSEN FOR ENGLAND

WRITING about Gosling, the banker, and Woodward, the architect, who were such great players in our game, I naturally began to recall the days when the amateurs were supreme.

The latter-day cynic may shrug his shoulders and flippantly remind me that they were paramount because there were no professionals. There is no reason why an amateur should not play football as well as a professional, save this, that physical fitness is part of the trade of the paid man.

The professional may be lacking in some technical points, but there is no justifiable excuse for unfitness. To be fighting fit, as the phrase in vogue expresses it, perfect condition is his job. An amateur cannot possibly be quite so healthy and in such good fettle, because he has other duties.

In some ways the high-class amateur has almost disappeared. I am not referring to social status, but to high-class play. This most unfortunate phase of modern Association football is the sequel to neglect and indifference.

The amateur was the controlling power in the national game, as he ought to be, long ago. Instead of fighting hard to retain his power through the 'eighties and 'nineties, he relaxed his grip, the reins fell from his hands, the professional clubs got the upper hand, and though they are a minority in number, they have captured the public mind until most people lose sight of the amateur, who is after all the salt of the sport and gives it flavour.

I wish I could rouse England to the importance of amateurism to the nation and to the country as a whole.

The reader has no right to be surprised because I say so. People are apt to forget that the F.A. look after all football and not a part.

That should have been the aspect of the situation to the amateurs of long ago. They didn't bother. They played their games and let the game as a whole, and in a political sense, take care of itself.

And now many, who under other circumstances would have been devoted to the Association game, are not with us. They are not taught to play this game while at school.

Everyone knows that since 1883, when the Blackburn Olympic, a club long since as defunct as the prehistoric animals at the Crystal Palace, won the Association Cup, no amateur team has ever even reached the Final tie for The Cup.

I have not forgotten Queen's Park, but they cannot be counted as domiciled in England, for their home is at Glasgow.

While the victory of the Olympic cannot be forgotten, as this triumph ended an epoch, how many remember that not even one amateur has received a Cup winner's gold medal since Kenneth Hunt had the honour in 1908, when he was a player in the team of Wolverhampton Wanderers—one amateur amid ten professionals?

Do you know, as counsel says, that Kenneth Hunt, then assisting Leyton, a professional team in the Southern League, was the last Corinthian who played for England, against Scotland in April, 1911, although another amateur, the late George W. Webb, of West Ham, the centre-forward, was his colleague?

Not a single amateur against Scotland for 23 years!

And since the European War the only amateurs who have helped England against the other countries, Wales and Ireland, have been A.G. Bower, B.H. Baker, G.H. Armitage, C.T. Ashton, J.F. Mitchell, K.E. Hegan, M. Woosnam, E.H. Coleman, and A.E. Knight—nine men since 1919.

They appeared in one or other of eight matches and I am glad to add that only one of those games was lost.

The Old Carthusian, Bower, was a capital and a calculating back.

At his best Howard Baker was a first-class goalkeeper and might have kept for Aston Villa, as an amateur of course, had his father not deemed it wiser for him to look after more pressing affairs.

In the 1925 match against Ireland, Baker was in goal, Armitage, an accountant, was at centre half-back, and Ashton at centre-forward. Not a goal was scored in the match.

Bower and Lieut. Hegan appeared against Ireland in 1923. Hegan was placed at outside-right in preference to any professional, whereas his best and customary position was at outside-left. That was the match that was lost.

Do not overlook the fact that Ireland had defeated England in both 1913 and 1914 against very powerful professional elevens. We did not lose in 1923 because there were two amateurs.

Again, Mitchell was a goalkeeper safe enough to play for Manchester City, and for Preston North End, like Dr. Mills Roberts did, in a Final tie for the Cup.

Coleman, of Dulwich Hamlet, was another who excelled as goalkeeper and he kept against Wales in 1921 and never made a mistake.

Max Woosman, like Ashton, was a Wykehamist who got his Blue at Cambridge, and helped Chelsea and captained Manchester City. He won the match against Wales in 1922 by placing a free-kick so exactly that R. Kelly, then at Burnley, was easily able to head the only goal of the match.

Arthur Knight, a fine back for Portsmouth, who would play with any eleven, a third eleven if need be, rather than miss his tonic, a game at football, was for a long time a Corinthian stalwart. He played against Ireland in 1919.

These were the men the Football Association were able to get even while professionalism was rampant, as our traducers prefer to phrase the situation.

But Bower, who played against Wales in 1927, was the last amateur to wear England's jersey in an international match!

The Football Association have been anxious to raise the standard of amateurism by inducing the Public Schools to revert to their old practice of promoting and encouraging our game.

The headmasters, maybe influenced by the games-masters, refuse permission to play our game, and thereby encourage the Rugby form of football.

There is a feeling, no matter how much it may be denied, that Rugby should be the game of the classes and that Association football should be left to the masses. To me this savours of snobbery. The pretext is the objection of the headmasters to professionalism. That does not appeal to me as a perfectly true explanation, and is clearly not approved by the schools that still adhere to our code of football.

There was a time when England had only amateurs, but since the professional was given a status the high-class amateurs have diminished in number, and as I have already shown, it is seldom that there is one amateur thought good enough to take part in a representative match. That is the result of this prohibition.

I have reason to believe that the parents of the boys are as anxious now as ever they were that they should play our game, and covet the honour attaching to their son's selection as an international. What chance has the boy when he is not permitted to kick an Association ball while at school?

When he leaves his Public School he has no knowledge of the game. He goes out into a world that is passionately devoted to Soccer, no matter where he travels, and he cannot play this great game that Great Britain has given to the whole world.

As one of our old stalwarts, John Lewis, used to say, as he banged his hands together, "It's a mess."

Perchance the boy goes up to the 'varsity. Now at Oxford and Cambridge the decline of Association football is deplorable. The University match, as it is known, has for years been poor stuff. The public takes no interest in these matches, which for a long time have not been worthy of two college elevens, let alone two elevens chosen from the universities. This is a great misfortune.

Many of these boys go into the Services—the Navy, the Army or the Air Force. Do we find the officers playing with their men? They have no knowledge of the game. It is admitted that this is regrettable. Commanding officers in all branches of the Services like to see games played by all, irrespective of rank.

Let us get back to the foundation stone of school sport. Give the boys freedom of choice, let them be taught Association football as before. Give the amateur the opportunity of coming into his own again.

I do not make these remarks to the detriment of the professional, but it is very delightful to spectators when the two, amateur and professional, are associated in the same games.

They should be associated as in cricket. How would England have fared in the long series of Test matches against Australia if there had not been amateurs to call upon? There amateurs and professionals have always been playing side by side.

Somebody says, "Oh, but cricket is different." My answer to that is that the private and domestic arrangements of clubs employing professionals have nothing whatever to do with boys playing a healthy invigorating game at school. One might as well contend that the boys at Public Schools must not be taught boxing, because there are professionals who meet and batter each other for vast sums of money.

There are people who do not want to know or to understand the good points of professionalism in football. There are many, but my point, now and always, is that we should endeavour to restore the prestige of England's amateur football and to obtain players of this kind good enough to play for the old country, to play skilfully and sportingly with our sailors and soldiers, with their fellow-workmen from the factory and the mine, and with any business house or ordinary club when they go out into the larger world.

At the time when amateurism was at its zenith the Corinthians had learned to play Soccer at the Public Schools, and when they went to the University, they knew the game. They don't now.

In the early days of the Corinthians, N.L. Jackson ("Pa"), their organizer, was a vice-president of the F.A. and a member of the Selection Committee. I can hear him saying, "Come and play for me and I will get you your international cap." And he did. And the Corinthians were proud of their caps.

Is it fair that the present generation should be deprived of these rights, privileges and honours at the dictation of the headmasters of their schools because of some objection to professionalism? Let the headmasters themselves state their reasons, and prove that Shrewsbury, Malvern, Winchester and other schools, the loyal minority, are endangering the morals of the boys entrusted to their care.

Of course, I have heard a thousand times the arguments, so called, about the commercialism of the Football Association, the white slave traffic in the professional side of the game, and various forms of cancer.

Many years ago, before Rugby football became such a fashion, a great deal was heard about what some personages were pleased to call the "gladiatorial phase" of the Association game. The players were compared with the gladiators of ancient Rome and the crowds with the mobs who went to the amphitheatre and the circus.

Those sights were seized upon as events preceding the fall of the Roman Empire. The decline and fall of England and the British Empire were predicted. Did anyone ever heard such bosh?

Since Rugby can attract 60,000 or 70,000 people to the Twickenham arena, the schoolmasters, the clergy, the professors of all sorts of "isms" are as silent as the sphinx about the gladiators and the sin of watching football.

"Why don't these fellows who go to Soccer matches play the game themselves?" That was the popular question among the critics. Nowadays that silly idle taunt is never heard. There are boomerangs among what some folks have been pleased to regard as arguments.

Very few sports are without spectators. I understand that even the golf links have been invaded by lookers-on, and from what I read some of them do not know how to behave themselves.

I should be horrified if the reader said, "Isn't Wall throwing his weight about?"—I believe that is the phrase. I had no intention of doing anything of the kind, but it is impossible to avoid feeling the silence of some of those who attacked the Association game.

There is plenty of room for every form of football. Let a man either play or watch the code that appeals to him.

The Football Association have not been in the habit of attacking the sports and pastimes that are the favourite recreations and amusements of other people.

The Association have considered themselves the guardians of their own game, have worked for the control of open and honest professionalism, and have done everything that they could to encourage and develop amateurism among all classes.

They may not always have had the support they hoped for, but the directors of the big clubs and the paid players have been men who have striven to keep a national game free from malpractices of all kinds.

The class of amateur who should have helped and co-operated with us has not been able to overcome its extraordinary prejudice, although I begin to believe that the cant and rant are declining.

Returning for a few moments to the commercialism with Which the Football Association is charged: What is the capital of The Football Association, Limited—the legal title of this body? The scheme drawn up by men who were as sound amateurs as any purist could desire, was that the capital should be £100, in the form of 2,000 shares of one shilling each, and that no shareholder should be entitled to any dividend, bonus or profit.

No dividend has ever been paid and can ever be paid without altering the legal foundations of the Association under the Companies Acts.

Someone will bob up with the question: "Why become a limited company at all?" This was done on June 13, 1903, not for the distribution of profits, but for the protection of the members, who are clubs.

The F.A. have never been concerned with profiteering, if I may use such a word, but funds are essential. I do not want to stress the point of the money that has been devoted to philanthropic and charitable causes, directly and indirectly, under the rules.

The F.A. had a balance of £2 17s. 5d. in 1875. The game became such a passion with all classes that in 1914 the investments of the F.A. amounted to about £15,000.

How money can disappear in the air and we cannot help ourselves! In 1917 that balance was reduced to about £2,500, in 1918 to less than £1,000. The Football League gave the F.A. £1,000 to help them along when the investments were reduced to £465.

Now there has been such a passion for sport since the war that the F.A. have become possessed of such a large sum as £100,000. Everyone is putting the question: "What are they going to do with it?" Some of it will be husbanded for extraordinary calls that have to be met.

This is a world of startling change. The F.A. have been advancing money to their members who wish to buy the freeholds of their grounds. They lend a sum not exceeding two-thirds of the estimated value of the land. They hold a mortgage, cannot lend more than £3,000, and the principal has to be repaid by instalments, plus interest at 3 per cent.

The F.A. give grants to affiliated associations as they may need, and they help in many other directions whenever appealed to. It is possible, perhaps probable, that it may be necessary to provide thousands of pounds per annum for the encouragement and teaching of Association football in Secondary Schools all over the country.

This is a new movement to which there is no limit. The F.A. wish to rouse the interest of the Secondary Schools and the Public Schools which have held aloof or have discontinued the playing of Association football.

If a boy plays at school he is likely to retain an interest in the game later in life. The game primarily needs those who love to play, but there comes a day when the player becomes the spectator. All who are connected with football desire more, and still more spectators.

It is necessary to plant the seed and to gather the harvest. Let it be said once for all that money is never "invested" in football for the purpose of dividends. It is put into it for the sake of sport.

Few clubs pay dividends and not one can be relied upon to do so. And when talking about commercialism, do not forget that the dividend is a limited interest without security.

And when superior persons talk about "slave traffic" it is well to remember that the slave has some voice in the matter of his sale. The professional footballer is neither a chattel nor a fool. He has the right to refuse to be transferred from one club to another and he has often exercised that right. Both famous and unknown footballers have declined to be transferred, preferring to remain with the club they knew most about. That is not commercialism.

CHAPTER VIII

INDIVIDUAL TRIUMPHS FOR
ENGLAND AND SCOTLAND

No satisfactory answer could be given to the question: "Which has had the greater influence on the game, the Association Cup or the International Tournament—and why?" I can imagine some expert putting such a question upon an examination paper relating to Association football. Possibly the student would wish the examiner to define the exact meaning he attaches to the word "influence."

The Cup ties have brought tremendous changes and have aroused much interest, nay, even excitement, among the general public who could not be described as football enthusiasts. These ties have helped in the development of clubs all over Great Britain.

This generation does not remember the period when Scottish, Irish and Welsh clubs entered and took part in the struggle for the Cup. Scotland and Ireland decided to retain their clubs for their own national knock-out competition, but the Principality never raised any objection, and eventually the Football Association found it necessary to limit and select the number of Welsh clubs wishing to compete.

The Cup made the game popular as a club attraction, and in spite of many innovations in our own and other sports and pastimes, the trophy of the parent body still pulls the people within the gates and endows the second half of the season with variety and life. The Cup has served its purpose and nowadays exercises more magnetic power than ever.

And yet all those who love football for its own charm as a

game, and not as a money-maker or a provider and creator of mass-excitement, must surely admit that the International matches, and especially those between England and Scotland, have exerted a tremendous influence, as these games have set a standard of play, have encouraged a pure sporting rivalry between the four nations of Great Britain, and have stimulated players to strive to improve their own game and thereby obtain the distinctions they covet.

The International matches have aroused and cultivated ambition in a national and individual sense. As they ought to set the highest standard of play in every respect, it seems unfortunate that the trend of modern club competition does not tend to maintain the paramount position and supremacy of the British championship.

The one match of this type that retains its pre-eminence, spice and character is that between Scotland and England. Indeed, I think that this encounter, even when played in England, makes a more vivid appeal than ever, and stands second only to the Final tie for the Association Cup.

As both matches found a place in the football calendar for 1872, they may be said to have given the world the model of a cup tourney for clubs and an example for friendly rivalry among the nations.

The first match between England and Scotland was played on November 30, 1872, at Glasgow, when the match was drawn without a goal being scored. The return took place on March 8, 1873, when England won by 4–2. It is a coincidence, almost always overlooked, that these games took place on the fine enclosures of the West of Scotland Cricket Club at Partick and the Surrey County Cricket Club at Kennington Oval. Each match was a great stimulus to our game.

When the first match at Partick was over, the Scots gave three cheers for the English eleven, who at once raised their voices to return the good feeling, in the old-fashioned way. Over the dinner-table in the evening the Scotsmen and their guests fixed the date for the encounter in the following spring.

One day I happened to discover the balance-sheet of this first international contest at the Oval. The gate money was £99 12s. and tickets sold in advance brought in £6 9s., the total receipts thus being £106 1s. When this match was last played at Wembley, on April 14, 1934, the F.A. received £13,384 18s. 5d., after the proprietors of the Stadium had taken their percentage of the revenue and met the ground expenses.

What did the F.A. do with this £106 1s.? The tiny balance-sheet sets out in detail the payments. Hire of ground £10, ground expenses £2, loan of tent £1, printing bills £1 5s., bill sticking 12s. 6d., printing cards 10s. 6d., cost of football 12s. 6d., Police 17s. 6d., luncheon to Scottish team £2 12s. 6d. and dinners to Scottish team £13 2s., the balance of £73 8s. 6d. going to the Association.

Evidently the English team entertained themselves and paid all their own expenses. When we compare these paltry sums with the Wembley match of 1934, when the F.A. expenses amounted to £524 6s. 11d., and when we think of the cheering and the dining, we see indeed that times have changed and customs with them.

Nowadays there is hardly any social side to football as between the teams of the match. The Association have in recent years entertained the Continental teams, who are so very hospitable when our elevens go abroad.

"The Football Annual" for 1873, produced by my predecessor, Charlie Alcock, records with pride that "no less than 3,000 passed the turnstiles during the afternoon." Just over fifty years later at Wembley there were nearly 93,000 people and the gate was £20,173. And at Hampden Park, Glasgow, in 1933, the match between these countries attracted 136,259 spectators.

Such figures make me wonder whether the Cup Final or the oldest of our international matches has exercised the greater influence on the game. Most people would plump for the Cup, but I am not so sure.

To play against England is the crown of every Scotsman's ambition. One can understand a young player being excited when he sees his name on the printed page, or cast on the screen of a picture-palace in Glasgow, but there have been Scottish players, experienced men engaged with English clubs, who have been so elated at their selection, as to become "mad for the moment." And this by the dour Scot!

The English footballer likes to get his "cap," the only one worth having, he says; but some of the Scot's ardent appreciation would make him all the better man in action.

When England and Scotland played in London the matches were for some years invariably allotted to Kennington Oval. The Surrey club having found that it became necessary to returf the centre of the ground, the committee thought it desirable that football should not be played there during the spring of 1893. Therefore the match was taken to the ground of the Athletic Association at Richmond, where so many leading Rugby Union games had been decided.

This rendezvous was popular and the gate, £811 exceeded considerably that taken at any previous Association international contest in England. The Scotsmen declared that they had never played in such spacious and handsome surroundings.

Among the company was the Duke of Teck, who was accompanied by his daughter, Princess May, now the Queen of England.

When their Majesties the King and Queen were so gracious as to attend the Final tie at Wembley in 1932, King George walked on to the ground while I conducted the Queen to the Royal Box. As we were going up the steps I said, "May I be permitted to recall a match at which you honoured us with your presence. It was played at Richmond." Her Majesty smiled and made answer, "Oh, that was a very long time ago." Yet the Queen remembered the occasion very well.

John Goodall, still living at Watford, was unable to play at Richmond owing to an accident. Nevertheless, the English eleven blended much better than was expected. Their stamina and speed served them well. Even so late in the match as after crossing over, the Scots were leading, but England won by 5–2.

For years afterwards the shrewdest judges in Scotland were convinced that this was the fastest match of the whole series. Until changing ends, Scotland held her own, but during the last half-hour, when R.C. Gosling established a happy understanding with W.I. Bassett, who was swinging the ball from outside-right to outside-left, the Scottish half-backs, James Kelly (the captain), Willie Maley, and David Mitchell had no pith left in their legs and "couldna run."

That's just how matches are won and lost. There comes a turning point—after a breaking point. During this season of 1892–93 England won her three international matches by so large an aggregate as 17 goals to 3.

Now five of these goals were scored by F. Spikesley, of Sheffield Wednesday, including three in this match at Richmond. He had played against Wales less than a month before the match against the Scots, who declared that he was a "regular flier." That he had extraordinary speed for a young man of his build is beyond doubt.

I should say, at this distance of time, that he was about 5 ft. 8 in., if that, and a light-weight. Long ago, when he was still playing, Spikesley was referred to as weighing 11 st. 7 lb. I should take two stone off that estimate, as he was a trim trickster, neat and slim and sure in all that he tried to do.

A native of Gainsborough, he played for the Trinity club, and went from that prolific nursery to Sheffield Wednesday. A natural footballer, if ever there was one, he had the advantage of playing both at Gainsborough and Sheffield with some Scotsmen who had the characteristic quality of their race—ball control.

Thus a youngster who could use either foot with equal facility had the advantage of developing his gift to the top of his bent. Whenever I saw him he played well, but never better than at Richmond, for he scored the three last goals in about ten minutes. I cannot recall any other Englishman obtaining three goals in a match against Scotland. It may have been done, but if so it happened before I was keenly interested in these big matches.

The Scots tried to keep the ball away from Spikesley, who had such a clever partner as Edgar Chadwick, at inside-left. Of course, all the credit for these three goals cannot go to Spikesley, for Bassett made long passes of much accuracy, and if Chadwick got the ball he gave his mate a perfect position.

Spikesley was so alert, so apt to anticipate the next move, and so quick that he baffled his opponents.

The Scots were insistent in their appeals for off-side, but Mr. J.C. Clegg, who was the referee, held that the goals were legitimate. Of course, there were people who did not agree with him. That has been the lot of the referee in every age, but, Mr. Clegg, who was not only a good and bold referee, but always trusted his own eyes, was well aware of the speed of Spikesley and where he was positioned when Bassett made his cross-kick.

The moment the ball left Bassett's boot Spikesley was off in a flash. He would trap the ball with his right and crash it into the net with his left. This seemed like one movement because he was so rapid.

Conjurers have sleight of hand. Let me vary the phrase and say that Spikesley had sleight of foot. He did most of his dribbling with the outside of the right foot.

I do not like making sweeping statements, but I have never seen so thoroughly competent an outside-left as Spikesley, who relied not on weight, or even on speed alone, but upon his craft and power over the ball.

When his playing career closed he devoted his thought, experience and energy to teaching football in all parts of the world, from Mexico to Mannheim, or some other place in Germany.

For ten years he played in representative matches for the F.A. and the Football League, and was never on the losing side. He was England's mascot; he has not had a successor and his fortune on the field has not clung to him in more material matters, for he had several trying accidents and was one of the many to whom the European War made such a difference in circumstances.

The Sheffield Wednesday club have been indeed fortunate to have had the assistance of such players as W. Mosforth ("The Artful Dodger"), F. Spikesley and Ellis Rimmer, all at outside-left. None of my young friends will forget how well Rimmer played against Scotland in 1930, another occasion when England won by 5–2. Rimmer scored two of them, but little Spikesley stands alone with his triplet.

And he made a gracious lady, who became Queen of England, wave her handkerchief as one of his three goals was scored.

I like browsing and purring—I suppose I ought to say crooning, to use a word that now has a vogue—over the matches between England and Scotland and the Final ties for the Association Cup. They restore pictures of old friends, old fights, and old facts that may have been forgotten, or never known to some of the younger enthusiasts. Perhaps I ought to write "fans" to be quite modern.

Much has been written about Fred Spikesley, because the scoring of three goals by any player in an international match is very rare. Scotland has had three players who have been able to do this.

The records of these matches have been rather erratically preserved. In official circles no minute is ever kept of the men who score; merely of the number of goals. Therefore I have had to dive into Football Annuals—a rare form of amusement to me, if it be amusement. These "Annuals," especially those of the long ago, so often omit what is required.

The names of scorers are left out, the idea being that there should not be any personal side to a team game. As one of the old Preston North End eleven used to say: "Someone would get a goal. It did not matter who, so long as it was done. Our goalkeeper did the rest. If we were tired or stale or lazy we would get a goal and then leave the game to the backs and Trainer, the prince of goalkeepers, as the newspapers called him. The newspapers in my day never published lists of the leading scorers—a practice that does no good whatever to the game."

I am just putting these remarks before the reader so that he may understand how it is that there are no reliable records of Geordie Ker, whom Scotsmen always claim to have been the greatest centre-forward that ever played.

Originally a back, he found his true position in the centre of the attack. He was a great dribbler and a crack shot, according to all accounts. Whether he ever got three goals for Scotland I cannot say, but the first record of anyone doing so is that of Dr. John Smith, when he obtained three goals at Sheffield in 1883, and England were defeated by 3–2.

Perhaps some readers have never heard tell of Dr. John Smith, who stood 6 ft. 3 in., and weighed 15 stone. I understand that he still resides in Kirkcaldy, and he must be about 75 years old. He played for his native village of Mauchline, Edinburgh University, where he took first-class degrees, Queen's Park, the Swifts (the London club of the Bambridges), and the Corinthians. There were days when he assumed the name of "Miller" for newspaper reports.

Dr. Smith was a lover of many sports, and in his day was a great forward, for he had speed and weight. The ball left his foot like a rocket, and goalkeepers had little chance against him. He was a Goliath, but was not the man to rely on physique.

Seventeen years passed before R.S. McColl obtained three goals against England on the ground of Glasgow Celtic. A great dribbler and a splendid shot, McColl was well served by Bobby Walker on his right and John Campbell, once of Aston Villa, on his left. Some of the Scots avowed that he was second only to Geordie Ker, but it seems well to remember his supports, and that England's backs, both injured and unfit to play, were doing their utmost behind a set of half-backs who did not realize expectations by any means.

I have no wish to minimize England's reverse, but it seems fair to say that James Crabtree, the right back, broke down in about a quarter of an hour, although he had given the limb a severe test on the day. And after Crabtree, one of the finest players of his day was crippled, the Corinthian, W.J. Oakley, had a collision with "Jack" Robinson, the goalkeeper, and suffered from concussion.

The remarkable part of the story is that Oakley played through the game as if he had been an automaton or a Robot worked by a man's brain. It was an amazing exhibition of the power of instinct; his faculties were so dulled and dazed that he was unconscious of what was happening, and when the match was over he actually asked who had won!

Crabtree said that he could not understand how a man could play so well when in such a state.

The passing of the Scottish forwards was most exact and gave McColl his opportunities. He seized them like an artist who combined the trick of stealing away and finishing with a mighty thrust.

It seemed to me that the sturdy McColl revelled in the chance of breaking away quite unattended and snapping a goal.

A Glaswegian, in the service of the Corporation of this great city, McColl became a professional for Newcastle some eighteen months after this match. After about six years as a professional in England and Scotland, he was reinstated as an amateur and embarked upon a highly successful business career in his native city.

Although he wears spectacles, the last time I saw him he still had the upright carriage that distinguished this honest and highly-skilled player.

A year or two ago he invited the men who played with him against England in 1900 to see this annual battle fought out again at the Wembley Stadium. It was an interesting gathering of men who had won against the Saxons.

I must not overlook the most recent exploit of this kind, for A. Jackson, of Huddersfield, the well-known outside-right, had, as a wing raider, the same experience as Spikesley.

This happened at Wembley in 1928, when England's back divisions were so disappointing. Two members of the Blackburn Rovers could not control his movements or check his advances. England suffered much worse than in 1900, and had no extenuating circumstances to plead.

Football is like that, for one of the charms of internationalism is that each season provides figures as varied as those of the kaleidoscope.

CHAPTER IX

TWO GREAT BLACKBURN ROVERS

PREPARING to leave the offices of the Football Association on the day that I handed the reins to my successor, I took a last look round, and paused at the large photographs of Vivian Woodward and Robert Crompton, and wondered if the old country would ever have their equals in the future.

There are no other portraits of single players on the walls at headquarters: only Woodward, representing the South and the amateurs, and Crompton, the hardy North and the professionals.

These two great representative footballers have always intrigued me. No one who saw them play can ever forget their chivalry and high skill. Perhaps it is not too much to say that Robert Crompton was always "Bob" alike to his friends and his foes, and to those who neither knew him nor ever watched him on the field of action. He was a remarkable man; more noted for deeds than words. His deeds were testimonials to his temperament.

The young enthusiasts of these days may think that I am putting praise on Crompton with a trowel, but let me assure them that the honour of being the only professional player in the portrait gallery at the headquarters of the game gives him a pre-eminence that is thoroughly deserved. The honour is unique.

There is one point that I must emphasize. Do any of us ever think of the influence that good professional examples can have upon the boys who go to the big matches?

Crompton, a native of Blackburn, was born during September, 1879, and as a boy attended a Board school before going to the Higher Grade school. At each of these institutions he played football, and was a back for the Higher Grade eleven.

As he had the gift of using either foot he appeared on either wing, although he preferred the right. He helped a team in which his father was interested, and a Church club in the Sunday School league.

I am reminded of these details of boyhood because it was at this stage that he saw such renowned backs as Johnny Forbes and Tom Brandon.

They were both Scotsmen of skill and style. And remember that he was at an impressionable age, and living in the midst of a countryside from east to west aflame with football.

Blackburn Rovers—with Accrington and Burnley to the east and Preston North End to the west—were midway in the sweep of the field, but with Preston a great rival, the matches between them were events that excited the local rhymester:—

> *When Rovers played North End,*
> *Tom Brandon did defend;*
> *He stopped Jack Ross*
> *From being a boss,*
> *When Rovers played North End.*

The Laureate of football has not yet arrived. But rhymes such as these were a vogue then, and they show how popular the game was.

The boy Crompton was a great admirer of Forbes, an old Vale of Leven player, who relied on his position play, his volleying and his pure football, but no doubt he learned much from watching both these backs.

Little did the boy dream that he would play in a match with Tom Brandon on his left. The Rovers have, so far as I remember, always had clever backs, and Crompton, with his natural gifts, imbibed their spirit and in some ways reproduced their touches. Boys are great imitators.

He was asked to join the Rovers while in his teens and consented. There was an idea of making him a centre half-back, as an understudy to Tom Booth, who played for England, and when he was chosen to play in the first eleven against Stoke and Aston Villa, during April, 1897, he appeared in that position, but he wished to be a right back.

And a full-back on the right he became, for with the usual man hurt he played in this position, with Brandon on the left, against Nottingham Forest. Success coming instantaneously, he was appointed captain the following season.

A man of one club, this great player, between Queen Victoria's Diamond Jubilee year and February, 1920, took part in over 500 League matches. His total number of appearances must be considerably more.

As the Rovers never reached the Final tie for 37 years, from 1891 to 1928, he never had the opportunity of trying to earn the gold medal awarded to the Cup winners. His career appeals to me more in the capacity of an international player than as an ardent club man.

Against Scotland, Wales and Ireland he had the unique distinction of playing 34 times, the record for his country. The Football Association presented him with his portrait—a perfect replica of that hanging at headquarters.

His record would have been increased but for an accident that placed him beyond consideration for the season 1904–05.

Of course, he captained England, and after the match against Scotland at the Crystal Palace in 1909, when he divided the honours with George Wall, who scored two such brilliant goals by his individualism, Crompton was presented to the Prince of Wales, now King George V.

In my opinion Crompton was the finest right back of his era, no matter what country is considered. His selection for international matches was automatic so long as he was in health and uninjured.

A heavy man—I should say he was 13 st. 7 lb. in his last match against Scotland in April, 1914—he was never speedy. His judgment, the position he took, and his patience and perseverance under all circumstances made him difficult to beat and pass.

No matter how the ball reached him, he could take it and

spurn it away with either foot. He placed his returns and made every effort to keep the ball in play by imparting screw. His idea was to serve his forwards and to keep the game going with a leg stroke that reminded one of a pull-drive at cricket.

He had to be in a very awkward position before he would put the ball over the touch-line. This was his last resource. He has even been accused of seriously endangering his goal by not taking the easier course.

Big and heavy as he was, he could "work" in little room. An adept at covering the wing forward so that to centre was seldom easy, he would wait and watch, run and watch, hamper and watch, for the forward to make the least mistake. If he did, Crompton had the ball. His intuition was uncanny and his tackle was timed to a nicety; to a split second.

With all his weight, he was never a man to rely on charging. He did not wish to charge light-weights, but he relished a bout with opponents who had fine physique and liked robust play.

How the Scots revelled in calling up men like James Quinn, George Livingstone and Bobby Templeton to give Crompton the time of his life! But they did not. If any Scot could charge Crompton to the grass, what a cheer he got! And what a compliment to the English back!

Thus the enthusiasts of pre-war football had the rare sight of a full-back who was comparatively slow being fast enough; who was heavy without making the most of his weight; and who preferred to play the ball and use it like a chess-master, rather than be fierce and mean in small ways.

He admired his foes. He once said that the best left-wing pair he ever faced as a combination was Peter Somers, of the Celts, with Howard McD. Paul, of Queen's Park.

They were "the hardest wing" he ever had to tackle, and the occasion was the inter-league match of 1909, at Glasgow Celtic's ground. The forwards of the Scottish League on that February day were: A. Bennett (Rangers), Bobby Walker ("Hearts"), James Quinn (Celtic), P. Somers (Celtic), and H. McD. Paul (Queen's Park).

I understand that five years after this match Crompton wrote a letter in which he said: "I shall remember them all, no matter how long I live."

Nevertheless, there is reason to believe that he considered Alec Smith, of Darvel, who played with Glasgow Rangers, the shrewdest and most skilful outside-left he ever met in an international match.

Since Anno Domini beat this Lancashire lad, the Football Association have never found his successor as a back. Between 1919–20 and 1933–34 England has had 11 right-backs, a full team, in his stead. Only three of them—Clay, of Tottenham, in 1922; Cooper, of Derby, in 1929; and Goodall, of Huddersfield, in 1931—have played in each of the three international matches in one season. And yet Crompton, save for a mishap, would have played for 13 consecutive years against Scotland.

Nor should it ever be forgotten that Crompton was a fair man. I remember West Ham United being drawn at home against Blackburn Rovers in the Association Cup ties of 1910–11.

If I recollect rightly, Butcher was the outside-left, and I could not help admiring Crompton in that match for the way he almost encouraged the winger. He often smiled at him as much as to say, "I like your style, but I shall stop you when I want."

A friend of mine, who was so very fast in his youth that he could have left this back standing still, once played against Crompton in a charity match at Blackburn.

In describing his experiences he said, "When I got the ball he gave me every opportunity. He ran near me as I was skirting the touchline. He said, 'Go on, young 'un,' and eventually whispered 'Now centre,' and I did. I wonder how many cracks would encourage a youngster like that."

There was once a keen match between Manchester United and Blackburn Rovers, at Old Trafford, when the right-wing raider thought he would try a fall with Crompton. He did—and fell.

As he regained his feet the forward shouted to the referee: "Penalty!" James Mason, of Burslem, the referee, merely said: "Superior strength," and went on with the game.

In the whole of my career I never heard anyone say an unkind or disparaging word about Crompton, and I hope that he is still taking an interest in football and getting some enjoyment out of life. He gave plenty to others when he was not in the corner of a railway carriage cuddling a "shilling shocker."

If Crompton never had the pleasure of receiving the gold medal as captain of the Cup winners, he was the skipper when the Royers became the League champions in 1911–12 and 1913–14. Brilliant as the Blackburn Rovers have been, only in these seasons have they carried off the great honour of the long club campaign.

If I were asked why they were supreme in these years, my answer would be another player's name— John Simpson, who has strong claims to be considered the cleverest outside-right who ever played.

This is an all-embracing statement that is likely to make the admirers of Bassett, William Meredith and Alec Bennett (Scotland has never had an Alan Morton on the right wing) jump up and protest.

I stand by "Jocky" Simpson, one of the only two real Anglo-Scots ever known, from my point of view. Of course "Anglo-Scot" was a term applied to Scots who took the high road south and played for English clubs in the League.

John Goodall and John Simpson were of Scottish blood, but, as it happened, born in England. In football law each was eligible to play for England, even though both learned their game north of the Tweed. They could rightly be described as Anglo-Scots.

The F.A. have never played a man in their national teams unless a member of an English club within their jurisdiction. Simpson was acknowledged to be the finest outside-right in Scotland, his club being Falkirk. Scotland could not legally play him. England could if they would.

In January, 1911, the F.A. went so far as to invite Simpson to take part in an international trial match, "Whites v. Stripes," at Tottenham.

The letter was sent to the secretary of Falkirk, Mr. William Nicol, and that happened just when Simpson had said that he would never again play for "the Bairns," as they are called. The reason why is of no consequence.

What happened I learned afterwards. Nicol went to see Simpson and found him in bed, owing to a headache. On hearing the news, Simpson said that he certainly would play at Tottenham, and he added that he did not intend to play again for Falkirk. Simpson could not be persuaded to alter his mind.

Nicol then wrote to Everton, Aston Villa, Sheffield Wednesday, Newcastle United, Bradford and Tottenham, saying that Simpson was for transfer.

Simpson saved the trial match from being an ordinary game, and he was signed the same evening in an hotel in Russell Square, London, by Blackburn Rovers, for the unprecedented fee at that date of over £1,800, of which it was said that Falkirk gave Simpson £500.

This was an outlay in those days, but it was largely owing to Simpson that Blackburn ran to the semi-final stage of our Cup in 1911. I am told that Crompton said "he got the money back at once."

England won the international championship of 1910-11, and it was a coincidence that the victorious eleven had Simpson, a Scot, born at Pendleton, Manchester, at outside-right, as well as Robert Evans, who had played ten times for Wales, at outside-left.

The F.A. discovered that Evans was born at Chester, and claimed his services, as they had a perfect right to do.

Simpson lived as a baby for some time at Pendleton, and Evans, who was born next door to Wales, was for three weeks at Chester. Still, the action of the International Selection Committee was thoroughly justifiable.

Truly, "Jocky" Simpson exerted considerable influence on the course of events in English football, although he was only with Blackburn Rovers for just over four seasons, the European war and an illness interrupting his brilliant career.

I have said that he was the cleverest outside-right I ever saw. Why? His control of the ball was such that it was very rarely any position was too difficult for him to use with advantage. His centres into the goal area were accurate from every possible position, and from some that looked impossible.

If he made a centre from the corner flag, or even volleyed from anywhere near the flag, he would use his instep so as to hook the ball back, and occasionally to curl the ball inwards to the goal.

Such centres made me say, "What a fluke," but when he did it three or four times in a match it became obvious that this was not just a lucky shot. His centres were about the best ever known.

In these times, with a relaxed off-side rule, much praise is bestowed upon a wing-forward if he scores freely. When Bastin got 33 goals in 1932–33 the figures were said to be a record.

All I can say is that Simpson got just as many under the old rule in a season at Falkirk. This club had then a class line of forwards, but it was Simpson's deadly left foot that scored so often.

And I remember that Woodward said that Simpson could do all he needed in a few inches. Most men would require a yard where he would be content with half a foot of space.

And he was so quick, not only in a sudden burst of speed to beat his opponent, but in using the ball to the advantage of his side.

Never was he selfish, because he invariably tried to make the right move. Born a footballer if ever a child was, he had no liking for any other game. Football was his only joy. He loved to be in the open air.

In his youth he began to work in a foundry, but he gave up indoor work, and when he was not playing about with a ball for a junior club, where he attracted a lot of attention, he was driving an omnibus between Falkirk and the village of Laurieston.

The Falkirk club heard about Simpson, and Mr. Nicol and Mr. Chapman, who was the librarian of the town, went out to see the youngster. They travelled by the omnibus that Simpson was driving. He heard them talking and making inquiries. Simpson knew who they were, but they did not know him.

When they got into touch with Simpson they recognized him as the laddie who had driven them to the village. They laughed at the joke and engaged him.

And in a year or so Simpson became "Wee Jocky Simpson," the football idol for miles round. Think of the feelings of some of the clubs when they saw this young man go to Blackburn. The Glasgow Rangers gave him a trial. Chelsea went North and offered £1,500 for his transfer. Newcastle United and Middlesbrough were just as eager.

At that time neither Simpson nor Falkirk would consider any offer. Simpson was happy among his own folk, and Falkirk knew his power over the public and other teams.

When the day came that Simpson wished to move, Falkirk could not understand his change of mind, because at that time he could be paid a higher salary in Scotland than in England.

Yet he came and conquered, although he was always a marked man. Nevertheless, he was an honest footballer, who gained the respect of his adversaries and won the admiration of the crowd.

CHAPTER X

FOOTBALL'S GRAND OLD MAN

I AM tremendously interested in people. Quinney, whom most of us know, seemed to divide or classify mankind into those who liked "persons" and those who preferred "things" made of stone, wood and other material. The first love human nature and the second cherish possessions. To me the most important study for man is mankind.

On the Football Association there have been all sorts and conditions of men. Some instantly make an appeal and awake a response that may be called appreciation. Occasionally, appreciation is superseded by a warmth of feeling known as affection.

Now "Charlie" Crump was a member of our football family, and, without gushing, I must say that we all loved the "old man," as we spoke of him in his latter days. He came on to the Council in 1883, and was made a vice-president in 1886, five years before Middlesex sent me to represent the county.

Nevertheless, in 1891 Crump was well known to the football community, if only for the hostility that he offered to the recognition of the player as a professional. As a worker all his life, he had no patience with the idea that a man should make a livelihood by playing football, which was surely a recreation after toil.

Looking to the end rather than to the beginning Crump saw nothing but the creation of loungers and loafers when their playing days were ended.

That is why he became so well known, although he had been a robust centre-forward, and a good referee.

Joe Chamberlain's monocle was famous. So was Charles

Crump's monocle. I am told that he played football while wearing his monocle. It seems impossible, but I have heard that this eye-glass sometimes fell, and that there was a hunt for it in the mud! I wonder! It sounds like a fairy story.

I want to tell you a lot about Charlie Crump. Another Wolverhampton gentleman, Tom H. Sidney, the nearest approach to Crump that ever I knew, used to tell a true tale about a funeral. Sidney said that he was walking in the east-end of London when a funeral procession, all the mourners on foot, passed. He stood still and raised his hat.

One of the mourners ran up to Sidney and exclaimed: "Thank you, sir, he was worth it." That is what I want you to exclaim when I have related the story of Crump.

When his son came home on leave from India he said to him, "I will show you a village where ten of us were born. I will show you a house where ten of us were born. I will show you a room where ten of us were born. I will show you a church were ten of us were christened. But there were not forty of us. Only ten of us, received into this world in the same room." The village was Kingsland, near Leominster.

The family removed to Shrewsbury and then to Wolver-hampton, where Crump remained for the rest of his life. For nearly 49 years he was connected with the Great Western Railway and was filling a highly responsible position when he retired on a pension.

While with the works of this company he founded the Stafford Road Football Club, and was one of the two centre-forwards who played. There were six forwards in those days, the usual wings and two centres.

Crump was the captain, and "Annuals" of the time tell me that the first match ever played between London and Birmingham took place at Kennington Oval, on December 1, 1877. It is stated that "the Birmingham team was very weak and the Cockneys won easily by 11 goals to nothing." Well, Crump was the captain and his partner in the centre was S. Page, of Wednesday Old Athletics.

The return match, decided a month later, was quite another story, as London only won by one goal, scored by P. Fairclough, of the Old Foresters.

These clubs can only be names or titles to most readers, but they must not imagine that Stafford Road was merely a very minor combination.

In 1880–81 Stafford Road had a memorable experience in the Association Cup. Having knocked out Spilsby and Grantham, scoring seven times in each tie, they received a bye and then defeated Aston Villa by 3–2.

In another publication, called "The Midland Football Annual," for 1882, this game is referred to in this way: "After a very one-sided match, all in favour of the Villa, and opposed to all book form, the Stafford Road stopped the progress of Aston Villa in the English Cup ties"—after the "Villans" had removed Nottingham Forest and Notts County, who were then the favourites for the Cup. Evidently the partial club reporter is not a product of these days.

This victory brought Stafford Road up against the Old Etonians, who only won by 2-1. The Old Etonians entered the Final and were just beaten by the Old Carthusians. Clearly Stafford Road had men of mettle if the club had no book form.

Crump, then over 40 years of age, was the captain of Stafford Road, and Lord Kinnaird, about seven years his junior, was the captain of the Old Etonians. I wonder whether that was their first meeting. I should not be surprised.

Kinnaird became our President and Crump our senior vice-president. And they died within a month or two of each other; Kinnaird on January 30, 1923, and Crump on April 15, 1923.

I suppose I may say that Crump died in harness. Whenever an international match is played by England the members of the F.A. Selection Committee are present. Crump, having been on this committee for many years, attended the drawn match between Scotland and England, at Hampden Park, the day before his death. After the game the F.A. party travelled to Edinburgh. Crump said that he did not feel well, and my wife and I journeyed with him and saw that he was made comfortable and rested.

At the match his interest never flagged, but he died suddenly the next morning—a Sunday.

He was in his eighty-fourth year and had been for forty years a member of the Association Council, and for forty-eight years the president of the Birmingham and District Association, and during all this time had wielded an immense influence for good after being convinced that professionalism was inevitable and must be governed firmly for the advantage of the sport as a whole.

It is because I am a lover of persons, as distinct from things, that I have found so much to admire in Charles Crump.

He was mistaken in his idea that professionalism would be the means of producing idlers. We have a fine type of man among the players of to-day. Doubtless he was thoroughly honest in his idea that the old player, past his physical prime, without any occupation, without a trade, and without any money saved, would be a pest, a hanger-on and a standing reproach to the policy of giving him a status in the game.

Of course there are ne'er-do-wells, but they are common to all classes, and the percentage among footballers is no larger than among men who have been trained for higher walks of life or among skilled artisans.

I have known and met thousands of players in my time, and have found very few scamps or men who shy at the mention of work.

Crump was himself a worker. No journey, no inquiry, no commission, no task that required the utmost care ever appalled him, even when he was advanced in years.

When he was eighty years of age he would rise at six o'clock in the morning, catch an early train, attend the last obsequies of some departed brother enthusiast for the game, and travel home again the same day.

He had the energy of a young man; indeed, many who were younger would not have taxed themselves as he did to show his sympathy and respect on such an occasion.

For many years Mr. Crump, Mr. Dan Woolfall, of Blackburn, and myself, acted as a sub-committee to revise the rules, regulations and bye-laws of the Football Association. Several times we gathered at Llangollen and at Shrewsbury, a town with old recollections for him.

If appointed on any commission of inquiry, he would examine closely into all details. He was anxious to find out the rights and wrongs of any matter.

If ever a director, an official, or a player was in trouble, often was the man known to say, "May Crump be my judge."

A friend of mine once said to him, "Mr. Crump, there is no definition of a charge in the laws of the game." "No," was the answer, "there are some things better without a definition. They are left to our common sense."

He was a vigorous player, according to his contemporaries, of the Kinnaird kind. He employed the charge with the shoulder in the good old way. What he lacked in stature he made up for by his activity and sturdiness.

And in his day referees were not so fastidious about detail. They knew that charging was part of the play and that the man who gave a charge took strength out of himself. There are two ways of looking at a charge. It is not all gain.

At any rate, Crump was not as gentle as Mary's pet lamb. Mr. George Ramsay, for so long the chief official of Aston Villa, once said to him: "It's a long time since I played my first match against you and I soon came to the conclusion that you were a rough man." The reply of Crump was, "When Villa and Stafford Road last met at Perry Barr something happened. I was not the only man who went off the field crippled, but I suppose you think that I crippled myself." These exchanges occurred at a club dinner and the sallies caused much laughter.

Charles Crump used to tell a tale about a man who played with The Druids, the renowned Welsh club of long ago. He said: "This man had only the stump of one arm, but he presented it to you—and then laughed."

There is really no reason why a man with the stump of an arm should not play again, especially as the truth-sayers (I wonder) have declared that a man with one leg and a crutch once kept goal.

There was a match, about 54 years ago, between Aston Villa

and Aston Unity, in which it was stated that the play was very rough indeed. So the newspapers said. Some of the players attended a meeting of the Birmingham Association and avowed that it was a pleasant and enjoyable game. The Association determined to write to the newspapers and say so.

Mr. J. H. Gofield, who was the honorary secretary, then proposed, "That under the auspices of the Association a match should be played in which 'charging shall not be allowed,' and that clubs should be invited to send representatives who are known to abstain from rough play." This proposition was carried, but whether the match was played, and if so the result, I cannot say.

Our game would be all the better to-day if the old-fashioned manly shoulder charge, with elbows close to the body, was revived.

Mr. Crump had what most of us would say was a unique experience. He played for Stafford Road in the first final tie for the Birmingham Senior Cup in 1877. His club was defeated by the Wednesbury Old Athletic. It was then his duty, as president of the Birmingham Association, to present the cup to the captain of the team that had beaten the eleven he led as their captain. He must have been the ideal loser to make a happy speech.

The same clubs met again in this local final two years later. The score was level at the end of ninety minutes, but Crump agreed to extra time, although there were two players disabled in his team.

He declared that this was a better plan than to allow so big a match to end in an unsatisfactory draw. Of course, Stafford Road were again beaten, but Crump's sporting spirit had been satisfied.

He was an excellent referee because he relied on common sense in interpreting the laws of the game. He was in charge of the Final tie in 1883, when Blackburn Olympic mastered the Old Etonians, who also agreed to an extra half-hour.

He refereed the match between Wales and Scotland at Wrexham in 1891. Scotland won by 4–3. The Queen's Park half-back, Tom Robertson, was the Scottish captain. Crump disallowed what looked like a goal. Robertson said: "Why was that goal disallowed, Mr. Crump?" "Now Robertson, get on with the game," was the reply.

When the match had finished, Robertson, who was walking off the field by the side of the referee, again put the same question. Always apt in stifling argument that had no purpose beyond satisfying curiosity, Mr. Crump answered, "Mr. Robertson, you have won the match. Be content." Of course, Tom Robertson went away laughing, but he never forgot the incident and talked about it as a model of diplomacy in later days when he became a highly competent referee himself.

In the middle of the 'eighties there was an excellent forward with Nottingham Forest. This man was deaf and dumb. He must not be confused with Tom Danks, who played against Scotland in 1885. "Dummy" Danks, as he was called, was his brother. "What a blessing it would be," said Crump, "if there were more players who were like him. Doubtless he got a lot of pleasure out of the game. Evidently, he enjoyed it and helped others to do so. The silent footballer is the best. As folks say in the North, he saves his breath to cool his porridge."

Although Mr. Crump had an infectious smile, was a man of bright eyes and geniality to the end of his life, he could be severe with any player who came before him for ungentlemanly conduct or who had violated the spirit of sport on the field.

His words lingered in the memory, and there used to be a story told of a young man in the Midlands declaring that he would sooner be suspended for ever than "lectured" by "Old Crump."

The fact that he was a member of the Emergency Committee of the Football Association, a committee endowed with almost as much power as the Council, and was also on the Appeal Committee of the Football League, shows what his contemporaries thought of his wisdom and his strict impartiality in all matters that came before him.

In the days before professionalism was legalized, football was played in Birmingham on the Aston Lower Grounds, a place of entertainment much more commodious than any club ground at that time. I remember the F.A. ordering a Semi-final Cup tie between Blackburn Rovers and Notts County to be played there in 1884. Notts County did not like the rendezvous, as there was then a very keen rivalry between Aston Villa and Notts.

These grounds belonged to a private company who were anxious to make money. That was natural. This company had an idea quite worthy of these days when there is a danger of football failing into the hands of commercial men who are speculators.

Eleven silver cups of the value of about £10 each were offered for a competition between a dozen clubs, who were to play on the knock-out plan, the winners of the tournament taking the eleven trophies for their own property, just the same as each man might have done at an athletic festival.

The reader may not see any harm in such a proposal, but there has always been a ban against the exploitation of the game by men who organize attractions for the sole purpose of making money.

This winter game must be solely carried on by clubs, duly authorised and strictly controlled by the Football Association and other similar bodies affiliated to it.

The money made by football, if any, must go into the till of the club treasurer and be used by him under rules and regulations for the benefit of the sport. Money must not be made for private purses.

The needs of clubs stand first and foremost. And rightly so. The Birmingham Football Association, with Charles Crump in the chair, at once decided that any club or player taking part in these "gate-money contests" should be disqualified permanently from taking part in any competition or matches organized by them. Crump said that his club was unanimously against such a rotten suggestion, which must lead to professionalism.

Of course, the trophies were never played for, but this is a very early example of the way in which football might have been collared by those who have no interest in the game itself, any more than they would have in soap works—except as a means of making money.

The members of the Football Association paid a unique compliment to the "Grand Old Man" on his 80th birthday, when he was as active as ever. The Association asked his acceptance of a cheque for £4,000, subscribed to a national testimonial in appreciation of his services and as an expression of affection and esteem.

The presentation was made at a banquet in 1920 by Sir Charles Clegg, who thought the world of Crump. He affirmed that no man had done better work for the game, and he added that he had never done anything in connection with football that gave him greater pleasure than to make the presentation.

To you these remarks may sound conventional, but coming from a man who never paid a compliment or offered praise unless thoroughly deserved, they conveyed a great deal. Sir Charles Clegg was deeply moved, and remember, he has very rarely betrayed emotion in public, whatever he may have felt.

I liked the tone of Crump's response, for he thanked Providence for good health and for a cheerful heart—gifts that had given him an abiding interest in real sport.

Except, perhaps, the national testimonial to Dr. W.G. Grace in 1895, on the completion of one hundred centuries in first-class cricket, it is doubtful if there has ever been a more spontaneous recognition of any leader in our two great national games. Crump was indeed a grand old man.

CHAPTER XI

THE CLUB DIRECTOR

UNTIL the Small Heath club, now known as Birmingham, was formed into a limited liability company for football, no one had ever heard of the word "director" in connection with the winter game. Small Heath was the first club to take this step, somewhere about 1888.

The innovation was not popular, but Small Heath merely anticipated a plan that was generally adopted in years to come and had much to recommend it from a legal and protective point of view. Mr. W.W. Hart, so widely known as an enthusiast, was the first chairman of the company, and one of the secretaries, Mr. Starling, in making application for admission to the Football League in 1892, contended that his club deserved such encouragement because they had been the first to introduce the limited liability company into football! That argument did not bring them sufficient votes for election to the First Division, but the club became members of the Second Division.

In this way the club "director" came into the game. The title was more imposing and attractive than that of "committee man." To say that a man was "on the committee of a club" was unimpressive and rather commonplace. To some the difference may appear small, but "director" at once implies a commanding position.

Nevertheless, a director has to hold a qualifying number of shares, and he takes upon himself liabilities and responsibilities that he cannot foresee.

Why does a man become the director of a club? Probably in his early manhood he played football and retained an interest in it when increasing years and cares prevented him from playing. He liked football and wished to remain in close touch with it.

Perhaps—one never knows—he wished to be regarded as "somebody," to have that little local elevation that is associated with being a town councillor or one of the leaders in any movement, even in football, which was not always a great game. Still, this form of sport developed rapidly and became national rather than local.

The man in the street, as the phrase runs, may look upon a football director as one who enjoys sitting in the best seats, the seats of the mighty, who attends all matches at the expense of his club, who has some chance of being chosen to represent the club or the district upon governing bodies of the game, and who knows at first hand those precious "secrets" that sooner or later become open secrets, or maybe involve him in troubles, the like of which he never anticipated. If he had he might not have become a director. There is some kind of a false glamour about being a director, for there comes disillusion, just as "behind the scenes" in a theatre may become an awakening to realities.

As the executive official to the Football Association for nearly 40 years, I have known many directors, and I am bound to say that they accept the duties, whatever they may entail, because they love the sport. That, in 99 cases out of 100, is true. They have no desire to obtain any reward beyond the success of their club and, through that, the success of the sport.

It may so happen, in a few instances, that a director becomes so infatuated with the game that his liking becomes an overpowering passion. His enthusiasm is such that he has only one point of view, and his club becomes more to him than sober judgment should permit.

I will not say that his conscience becomes blunt, but less sensitive. He will stretch a point for his club, and may break the rules and regulations of football.

A man who gives himself up to football, body and soul, as men do in other spheres besides this game, will take risks and get himself entangled in such a way as he would never dream of in the conduct of his own business. I write of what I know.

I have known directors who could not watch a match. They would go and walk about outside the ground, or in the recesses under the stands. Their heart was not strong enough to withstand the excitement. They are not with us now.

A director has been known to consider the question "to be or not to be?"—and to have decided "not to be." Others have ruined their business or spoiled their professional career. They have given themselves to the game and paid the penalty.

When Newcastle United was in its infancy, or perhaps before the rivals, Newcastle East End and Newcastle West United, joined forces, the pioneers, who were merely "committee men," used to meet under the big lamp-post in Gray Street, pool their resources, pawn their watches, or borrow money to pay the railway fares for the next match involving a journey. At least, I have heard this story told.

It may sound pitiful. Some may say: "What fools!" That may be, but the builders of football 50 years ago made great sacrifices. Those times had best be forgotten.

We are the beneficiaries. And their successors are the directors of to-day. But the reader shrugs his shoulders and says: "Directors do not have to pawn their watches in these days."

No, but we know directors, even in this century, who have poured tens of thousands of pounds into clubs. They are familiar to Yorkshire, Lancashire, London and other centres. Some have been repaid, wholly or in part, and some have not. Some enthusiasts are still emptying purses and unloading wallets.

Apart from giving thought and time to a club, directors have to undertake financial responsibilities. Before banks will permit clubs to have overdrafts they insist upon directors signing as guarantors for large amounts. Directors have had to supply the summer wages of the players.

Remember that there are more clubs with restricted revenue than those with ample resources. In football it is true that the poor are always with us.

Rich men, whose hobbies are yachting, racing, hunting, fishing and shooting, may spend as much or more upon what pleases them, but the generous football magnate gives, or helps to give, pleasure to thousands.

A few men have been bold enough to try to run a club of their own. The Football Association has always been opposed to "one-man" clubs. This is not the accepted idea of a club, which is supposed to represent the desires of a district, to be a joint effort by residents who have clubbed together for a common purpose.

The "one-man" club generally brings trouble, for the one person desires to make his own rules for the conduct of his own club. It may be his idea of making money.

Directors do not make money out of football, and they are more likely to lose than gain. They may do neither and still have a peck of trouble. Before we—you and I—talk about trouble, let us grasp once for all the thankless nature of a director's office.

When clubs formed themselves into limited companies the Football Association, between 30 and 40 years ago, drew up certain regulations for their guidance. There were two main principles, the limitation of dividends to 5 per cent., and that directors should not be paid, any more than any other shareholder.

This means that they get nothing for fulfilling that office, with all its duties.

The original regulations read: "A director shall not be entitled to receive any remuneration in respect of his office as director," but for the season of a 1927-28 there was an important addition, the rules reading: "A director shall not be entitled to receive any remuneration in respect of his office as director, or as an employee of a club."

The F.A. have always been convinced that if a director did not care to give himself for love of the game, the game was better without him. It is a job, to write plainly, with more kicks than half-pence. That is just the situation.

And yet directors have come under the ban of the F.A. and suffered suspension, some having been put out of the game for ever. The finding may seem severe. It may be urged that every punishment should have an ending.

So far as I am aware, those directors who have broken the

rules of the Football Association have not helped themselves to club revenue. These men do not enter the game to pilfer. If they want to get rich quickly, football is not for them. There are other ways and means that cannot be discussed here; they are not material to my subject.

The director has invariably got into trouble for paying players money that they were not entitled to under the regulations. For instance, let me quote a disastrous example.

In 1904, Manchester City won the Association Cup for the first time. I may say that this was a Pyrrhic victory. What happened?

Two years afterwards, it was found that Manchester City had made payments contrary to football law to their Cup team and some reserve players. Of course, they were dealt with and forbidden to play for the club at any time.

But, and this is the point I want to make, the whole of the directors, save one, were suspended. They valued their players more highly than they were allowed to do by the rules of the Football Association, who at that time fixed a maximum wage and forbade any bonus. What the club did was not an offence against the law of the land but a breach of the rules which all clubs were expected to keep.

This has always been the source of trouble, for as far back as 1893, at the annual meeting of the League, it was contended by the rich and powerful that the weak and poor were trying to be dictators, and that as the players made the money they had the first right to it.

That was only partially true, as the policy of the F.A. has always been: "Live and let live."

That is why directors who have ignored the scheme of payments adopted by all clubs have been banished for ever or otherwise severely punished—with a view to deterring the rich who, in those distant days, adopted many expedients for getting money that could not be traced as illegal payments.

Receipts for work never done and for goods never delivered enabled some directors to obtain funds for illicit payments to the men on their staff. In any case, whatever was earned by football did not go into the purses of the directors, but into the pockets of the players and for the provision of better accommodation on the grounds of the clubs.

The F.A. strove for honesty, the greatest good of the greatest number, and had their own way of ordering finance. Some directors had other plans and were dealt with for disobedience. Finally, there was a general amnesty for all clubs on the condition that they were righteous, in a football sense, for the future.

Eventually the F.A., becoming so weary of detective work in relation to payments to players, who, like Oliver Twist, were all asking for more, handed over the whole domestic arrangements of the League clubs, so far as money is concerned, to the League itself, the proper body to look after all such matters.

This was a wise move. There have been very few irregularities since, and directors can now sleep unless the bogey of relegation rears his ugly head. Why should any man ardently desire to be a director?

Someone has asked me this question: "Why are the best football brains debarred from directorates? Men like Wedlock are not permitted to become directors, while butchers, grocers and their like, with superficial knowledge, are allowed to be on directorates." I have been attracted to the subject by this questionnaire.

The first point I have tried to make is that the director holds an honorary position and has often brought trouble on himself by endeavouring to assuage the professional's thirst for gold. I admit that his thirst is not greater than that of most men, but the professional, who has chosen his own livelihood, is asked to conform to rules, regulations and bye-laws, and in his agreement and on the forms he signs he promises to abide by the conditions.

His outlook is generally entirely financial so far as this game and his participation in it are concerned. The Football Association, knowing something about human nature, saw that this would be so when the paid player was given a legal status.

One of the first rules the Association drew up in 1885 was:

"No professional shall be allowed to serve on any Association committee or represent his own or any other club at any meeting of the Football Association."

Later this rule was made more far-reaching. It was agreed that: "A professional shall not be allowed to serve on the Council of this Association, or on the committee of any association or club, or represent his own or any other association or club at any meeting of this Association, or of an affiliated association." That is quite comprehensive and clear.

Practically, that was the law of the F.A. from 1885 until 1903. Then, perhaps, some of the leaders of the F.A. thought that there were men who might be admitted to offices of this kind, and therefore the rule was re-cast once more. The text was framed thus: "A professional shall not be allowed to serve on the council of this Association, or on the committee of any association, league or club, or represent his own or any other association or club at any football meeting. When any person gives notice in writing to the secretary of this Association that he has ceased playing football, the council may, if they think fit, exempt such person from the operation of this rule."

The only change since 1903-04 is that "neither a professional, nor a professional reinstated after April 30, 1924, shall be allowed to serve," and so forth.

Clearly, for over 50 years the Association have been determined to debar professionals, as a whole, from taking any part in the government of this game. Nevertheless, about 30 years ago the Association endowed itself with the power to exempt anyone they thought fit.

The objection is not taken to any professional as a man, but to the principle that a paid player, or one who has been such, should take part in the government and control of the game, as that means the professional ruling the amateur.

The radical law in every sport, for its own good, is that the professional in status is subordinate to the amateur. The reader may ruffle his hair and call this doctrine antiquated or obsolete.

A principle, if it embodies truth, can never be antiquated or out of date. The truth is that the amateur, who should have no axe to grind, and no interest save that of the good of the game as a whole, is the more likely to be free from any ties and to have a mind that is not fettered by money or any financial consideration.

Professionalism has never been a success without rigid control, because the power of money becomes too strong. Jockeys are not elected members of the Jockey Club, and professional cricketers are not made members of the Marylebone Cricket Club. The question is not one of class but of control.

Doubtless some will say that this is nonsensical in these democratic days. Truth is unchanging. This is not a question of Wedlock *v.* The Greengrocer. Wedlock became a professional, and by so doing forfeited his right to rule. He might be a first-class legislator for anything I know.

Every one of these applications is decided on its merits. For instance, Mr. Phil Bache and Mr. William Bassett are on the Council of the F.A. Unless my memory is at fault, Mr. Jack Sharp, Mr. Richard Pudan, Mr. Robert Crompton and Mr. A.C. Jephcott have been on the directorates of Everton, Leicester City, Blackburn Rovers and West Bromwich Albion respectively.

Nor must I forget Mr. Howard Spencer and Mr. John Devey, who have been for so many years directors of Aston Villa. The football knowledge of these former players must be most valuable to the bodies they are associated with. No one can deny that. They have been thought fit. They are outside the pale of discussion.

I cannot imagine that anyone would wish to discuss them. They might want to praise their play, but only those who have sat in committee with them, and have worked with them, can assess their usefulness. They would be superior as players to the grocers, but it does not necessarily follow that they would be better organizers, as keen in debate and as far-seeing in judging of the ultimate effect of an innovation or a change of rule.

There have been other professionals quite as eligible, I should say, from what I have seen of them, to be allowed to take part in the management and control of the game. Wedlock always appealed to me as a natural gentleman, and such men as

Colin Veitch, of Newcastle; Harold Fleming, of Swindon; Evelyn Lintott, of Bradford City; James Lawrence, of Newcastle; and Charles Buchan, of Sunderland, readily spring to mind as men of parts. They should be welcome in any football company.

There again every man must be judged on his merits as a player, on his standard of personal conduct, and on his presumed fitness for committee work, where everyone is tested at close quarters.

The Football Association, as such, cannot be blamed if some district associations, or other organizations, choose unknown men for the Council—even if they elect butchers or grocers.

These people are not to be despised. Butchers and grocers supply our needs, and they may be first-class club workers who, by their zeal and sustained effort, have done much for the game in their own locality.

They may be even as good as a player who has taken every pound he could get out of the game until he became too slow. He has become old and cunning, as folks say.

Possibly his influence in the council chamber or at the round table might not be so wholesome as that of the blunt butcher and the suave and sugary grocer.

.

CHAPTER XII

FOOTBALL FINANCE

THE financial side of Association football is probably talked about on every day in the year. It is a topic of conversation in the market-place and in the Houses of Parliament. The vast majority of those who discuss this phase of a universal game seem to know very little about the subject.

Too often partisanship is confronted by prejudice. Essential points are never mentioned because of the ignorance that prevails. The partisan can see no wrong and the bigot contends that nothing is right.

Let me endeavour to enlighten both parties in the debate, and make an appeal to reason for judgment on facts.

I have seen the game grow from the pastime of enthusiasts, who played for the sake of exercise and amusement, to a national game that interests His Majesty the King, the patron of the Football Association, as well as the most humble of his subjects.

I can claim to take a dispassionate view, as an official of that Association for many years; an Association that have always endeavoured to adjust the balance as between amateurism and professionalism.

I have no axe to grind, and after being behind the scenes, I am in a position to express views that are fair and without the least bias.

I believe that there is no national sport more rigidly controlled than that of Association football in England.

There are those who hold that one side of our game, the professional branch, is a business on a purely commercial basis.

They are welcome to their opinion, but apart from the honest desire to pay all just dues, the leading clubs, whether they engage professionals or not, have no desire to make money for the sake of money.

The Football Association is nominally a limited company, but any idea that this is a trading company is nonsense.

Do you know a limited company like the F.A.? As I have already said, the capital consists of £100 divided into 2,000 shares of one shilling each. These shares are held by clubs—the members of the Association and the units of football.

The shares are not available to the public. No person can hold more than one share. No capital is called up and no dividend, no bonus and no profit is ever paid on them.

The F.A. is a limited company and as such its liability is limited under the Companies Acts. It exists for the benefit of football, and not for the benefit of the individual or the members. It is no more a "trading company" than a church or a philanthropic organization.

The very funds of the Football Association are held in trust for the good and the needs of the game. The Association is constantly appealed to by men who are workers for the common weal, for all kinds of causes and organizations, for help when great disasters occur in England and other parts of the world.

Only one who has been concerned with the administration of the F.A. has the remotest idea of the daily requests for grants and for aid, not only by institutions and agencies of repute, but by cranks who appear to think that football is the universal provider of funds.

The public are fully aware of the donations and subscriptions that the F.A. have made for many years. Much of the money that goes into the treasury of the Association goes back to the game in one way or another, and especially for the encouragement of amateur football. A man once wrote to the F.A. suggesting that a penny should be taken from the admission fee of every spectator at any match, for a certain national movement. No doubt he was honest and his idea was worthy of consideration as a theoretical project, but the F.A. had no power, no authority, to take any part of the gate money paid to clubs.

The Football League controls all the internal monetary arrangements of their clubs, but even those arrangements have first to be passed by at least three-fourths of the votes given by the clubs. The arrangements then become laws to be administered by the League.

If the Football League govern their own purely domestic concerns, it must not be forgotten that the F.A., as the guardians of the game, administer principles that apply to all their clubs.

As has been said, all the directors of clubs are honorary officials.

The capital of clubs is generally small and the dividends paid to shareholders, when they are earned, are limited to 7½ per cent. This fixed rate was originally 5 per cent. and was only raised after the war. With money so "cheap" as nowadays, it would not be surprising if the maximum of 7½ per cent. were reduced.

A big club always wishes to own the freehold of the ground, to equip it with large stands for the comfort of spectators, to keep their estate and stands in good condition, and to have a considerable staff of competent players as well as officials and other workers.

If to pay twenty shillings in the pound to everybody, including the police, the gate-men, and the band be described as a "commercial basis," then I agree that these words are applicable.

There are, however, too many limitations in football for the ordinary investor, and no sane person would ever dream of hoping to make a fortune out of football. Apart from limited dividends, there is far too much risk to be undertaken.

The main objects of all are to maintain the game as a sport, as a healthy recreation for all those who take part in it, and to provide an out-of-doors entertainment for the peoples of the world. This is the fundamental principle of our sport, but the development has been such that no one could ignore the financial side.

It is a common observation that money rules the world. Money is even necessary for providing recreation and entertainment, but remember that football has altogether outgrown itself as an inexpensive pastime.

Let us look back and sketch this extraordinary development. Even when football was played on open fields or public spaces it became necessary to rope off the pitch. In the days of one's youth there was no gate money.

However, it was necessary to have a groundsman and he required to be paid. We found that that had to be done even in the primitive days. Eventually we had to make a small charge of threepence or sixpence to admit to the matches. As the number of people began to increase, fences had to be placed round the grounds that we rented. Finally, clubs saw that there must be stands of some sort and an open enclosure in front of the stands.

We can visualize the growth from those early days to the present time, when clubs will spend from £40,000 to £80,000 on the erection of stands for the accommodation and comfort of spectators.

A number of clubs have to employ a ground staff as well as a clerical staff. Some of the premier clubs maintain a Works Department, and other clubs of lesser degree must have workmen employed on the general upkeep of the ground.

I suppose that very little thought has been given by the general public to the increase of expenses and the vast amount which is now spent on upkeep by constant attention to the turf and the repair of stands, dressing rooms, a gymnasium, a suite of baths of all kinds, a set of offices for the transaction of business, and the provision of trainers, doctors and paid prospectors who are always travelling about to look for both experienced players and recruits. The organization of a big club is greater than is generally understood.

Sometimes it is said that clubs make excessive charges for admission and for seats, but the only object in view is to provide accommodation so that the spectators of these matches shall see the game played under proper conditions.

Remember that all this is done and paid for out of the revenue obtained each season, and not out of the company's capital, which is generally merely nominal.

The late Mr. Herbert Chapman used to say that he had only eight months in which to make the £100,000 per annum he needed to pay for the purchase of the ground, spread over a term of years, for the construction of stands, for taxes and rates, and for the provision of new players as well as for the salaries of the older players and a large general staff. He had to maintain and look after a large estate as well as manage the playing of football.

Perhaps the reader may understand more clearly what faces the manager of a first-class club when I say that the purchase of the Highbury estate alone cost £48,000 and that the stand accommodation has entailed an outlay of at least £70,000. Such figures are appalling, I know, but it seems to me that people should know what a club has to face.

I am not in a position to speak with authority and in detail about Everton and Aston Villa, but their expenditure on grounds and equipping them must also have been very large.

Yet there are those who say that all the gates of League matches should be divided equally between the two clubs after payment of expenses, as in the ties for the Association Cup.

No mention of gate money, or expenses of any kind, is included in the original rules for the Cup competition. When the rules were revised in 1883 by the late Mr. Norman C. Bailey, a rule was introduced for the first time relating to gate money being shared equally, after deducting expenses.

Our predecessors had no idea of what the growth of the game would be. The expansion of football, even in relatively modern days, has exceeded the expectations of the most sanguine, and has entailed heavy responsibilities upon clubs for the safety of spectators when they have once entered the grounds.

I am not in favour of the gates of League matches being shared on an equal basis.

Let us take Everton and Millwall as one pair, and Arsenal and Swindon as another pair. We must consider the enormous expenses, the overhead charges of Everton and Arsenal, and the capacity of the grounds provided by these clubs out of their own funds.

It would not be equitable that the forethought and enterprise of the governing bodies of these and similar clubs, and the expenditure which they have been compelled to incur in providing for 60,000 or 70,000 people, should not bring them a great return. They are only receiving the just reward of their bold management.

There has not been the same demand upon Millwall and Swindon as upon Everton and Arsenal. It has not been essential for them to provide such spacious terraces and seating accommodation. It suffices for Swindon if they have a ground that will hold 20,000 people. Clubs such as Millwall and Swindon would, on the principle of equal shares, be receiving so much money that they would not know what to do with it.

The obligation has been placed upon Arsenal, Manchester City, Everton, and such clubs, and they have striven to meet it. The amount of their annual liabilities must be four times in excess of that of the minor clubs mentioned, and it would be an undue hardship upon these premier clubs were they compelled to pay any larger percentage than that which the League clubs have themselves voted—namely, 20 per cent. of the net admission money.

Again, consider what nonsense is talked about the transfer system of the Football League. This has been condemned with a contumely that arises from ignorance. The critics of the transfer system talk about the "buying" and the "selling" of human beings, in a manner that is harmful and prejudicial to the game.

Those who express themselves in such decided language do not understand the true position and have, with wanton abuse and malicious phrases, attacked the good repute of the game.

I am aware that the F.A. tried to pass a resolution in 1894 that "no club shall be allowed to receive or pay any sum of money as a consideration for the transfer of any player," but the motion was not carried.

Then, in November, 1899, Sir Charles Clegg, Mr. C. Crump, and Mr. C.W. Alcock presented a report declaring that "the practice of buying and selling players is unsportsmanlike and most objectionable," but a month later these gentlemen were asked to think again and report.

All the prophecies of the baneful effects of the system have been falsified. The system has proved sound in operation. It killed poaching by clubs for new men, and intriguing by players for fresh situations.

In a competition such as the League conducts, it is essential that the clubs should have a sense of security in their players, for that means a permanent team. To keep their best men is the desire of every club. The system gives them a hold upon them.

If Manchester United desire the services of a footballer with Aston Villa, the United must first ask the Villa whether he can be obtained, but the man required is not obliged to go, even if the clubs agree.

The consent of the player to any transaction is essential. Without his signature nothing can be done. He is a free man, not a bond slave, not goods, not a chattel. He has his rights. Moreover, he has a fixed salary the year round, and that means summer wages and three or four months' holiday. These summer wages are paid because the club holds his transfer and the directors have faith that his services will be at their disposal in the future.

The transfer system and summer wages are intimately related, and as soon as any player becomes attached as a professional to a good League club he is given a standard salary, a standard that he would not get without the transfer hold that the club has.

Football players are not merely playthings to be moved about at the will of their clubs.

The professionals have never, so far as I know, demanded the abolition of either the transfer system or the fee. They would not be human if they had not desired a larger share of the fee.

The Association once had the idea that no fee should be demanded above the sum paid by the club in acquiring the player, but later it was recognized that the club had a right to compensation for the loss of the services of a man whose play they had improved—the reason why his transfer was asked for—and whose place would have to be filled.

It was the loss of the player's services and the necessity of obtaining another to take his place that caused the first fee to be asked.

As a matter of curiosity, it would be interesting to discover who first asked for a transfer fee and who paid.

When the late Mr. John Allison, of Manchester City went to Preston and asked the North End for John McMahon, that picturesque right back, he was asked £450. In spite of the indignation that he affected, the money was paid. That happened, I believe, in December, 1902.

Let us note how the fee for the transfer of service has advanced:— £1,000 in February, 1905; £2,000 in November, 1913; £2,600 in March, 1914; £3,600 in March, 1920; £4,000 in November, 1920; £4,750 in February, 1921; £5,000 in February, 1922; £5,500 in March, 1922; £6,560 in December, 1925; £7,500 in April, 1930; £10,340 in October, 1928, and £10,775 in June, 1934.

It is admitted by all concerned that Middlesbro' paid £1,000 to Sunderland for Alfred Common, in February, 1905. On New Year's Day, 1908, the F.A. rule limiting transfer fees to £350 became operative, but the clubs so easily avoided the limit that four months afterwards the rule was rescinded.

Prior to the War it was generally believed that Manchester City paid the highest fee, £2,500 to Derby County for Horace Barnes, on May 12, 1914, but the late Robert Middleton, of Blackburn Rovers, used to take a secret pride in the fact that his club's £2,600 for Percy Dawson, the centre of the Heart of Midlothian, about two months earlier, was the "record."

The representatives of the clubs, Mr. Middleton and Mr. E.H. Furst, then a conspicuous man in the sport at Edinburgh, argued the night long.

And just when the President of the Football League, as soon as the War was over, was hoping that the continual advance of these fees would stop, Birmingham paid considerably over £3,000 each for J.C. Lane, of Blackpool, and John Crosbie, of Ayr.

It was in November, 1920, that Everton were credited with receiving £4,000 for the transfer of Stanley Fazackerley to Sheffield

United.

Some people gasped, but in the following February Preston North End were believed to have paid £4,750 to Kilmarnock for I. Hamilton, the back.

Within twelve months West Ham asked Falkirk £5,000 for the passing of Puddefoot, and to their amazement the money was paid. The terms were intended to be frightening and prohibitive figures.

Since then prices have leaped higher and higher. The £5,000 was more than doubled when Arsenal secured David Jack for £10,340 in October, 1928, and even this colossal sum was surpassed in June, 1934, when nearly £11,000 was the amount that Aston Villa gave Portsmouth for the release of James P. Allen, the centre-half-back.

Thus we see the advance from three to five figures, but really the amount of money that passes does not affect the principle that I have set forth—of compensation to the transferring club for the loss of a capable player and the provision of the means required to obtain his successor.

The fact that such large transfer fees have been paid has from time to time been severely criticized, but in my opinion the position has been caused by the responsibility placed upon the directors to satisfy the desires of their followers and spectators.

The directors, who are responsible for the welfare of the club, arrange for the transfer, and the directors, who receive this compensation in cash, do not get any benefit.

The true position has not been understood and the outstanding fact is that the transferring club, in their turn, entirely expend the money received in providing players and paying their wages.

The only objection that I take to the transfer system is that when a club has no use for a player, it does not provide that he should be given a free transfer to enable him to get another situation.

The clubs should not possess the right to retain a man on their list of players without payment of wages. "Live and let live" is a splendid motto.

CHAPTER XIII

THE F.A. AND AMATEURISM

THE Football Association have so often been accused of indifference to, if not neglect of, the amateur side of the game, that it becomes imperative to place in true perspective the relations of the parent body to all phases of the game, to the whole game and nothing but the game. I need hardly remind those who have even an elementary knowledge of the rise and progress of this sport that the Association, backed by a few enthusiastic pioneer clubs, established a cup competition to develop the playing of our game and its popularity.

The impetus was amazing; far greater than anyone could have imagined, especially as the game bounded into public favour in the provinces, particularly in the North and the Midlands. Big gates for the Cup ties, the intense rivalry of local clubs, and the importation of skilful players, who were secretly paid for their services, eventually brought such a wave of professionalism that the Association had not the power to prevail against it.

It was thought wiser to control the sudden development than to allow this giant growth to pass into other hands, and probably to a professional organization. That seemed inevitable, and therefore the leaders of the game accepted the vote giving recognized status to the professional, and prepared to rule both amateur and professional sections. Broadly, without entering into controversial matters, that is the position that arose.

From the day that the paid player was given legal status he has been placed under all kinds of restrictions. Some have disappeared, and some have been modified, but others remain. The dominant idea has been that the professional should not have a voice in the ruling of the game and in framing regulations for the conduct of amateurs.

To the end of the season of 1906-07 the first rule of the Association read: "The Association shall consist of such clubs and associations playing Association Football, and being otherwise qualified according to the laws, rules, regulations and bye-laws of the Association as the Council may approve."

For the season of 1907-08 this rule was extended. There was an addition of two sentences, the text being: "Affiliated Associations shall, when necessity arises, admit to membership both amateur and professional clubs within their area, and provide for the proper management and control of such clubs. The management of amateur and professional football may (if desired) be carried on in sections." These words have remained unaltered.

The first of the two new sentences was in a large measure the cause of what was called "the split" and the founding of the Amateur Football Association. The second sentence has never been acted upon, either because there was no real reason for so doing, or because there was a feeling that such an arrangement would be cumbersome, if not most difficult, to work in committee and in detail with smoothness and satisfaction.

Besides, the unity of the body was a state that appealed to both sections during the years that have since passed. The Association could be so divided, *if desired*, but apparently there has not been that desire. Nor do I feel that there has ever been such a necessity in my time.

As already said, there were restrictions upon professionals, who were at first not allowed to compete in the Cup ties without a birth certificate qualification, or residence for two years within six miles of the ground or headquarters of the club. This idea, obviously based upon the rules of first-class county cricket, proved inapplicable and, as we all know, the professional teams gained such an ascendancy in the Association Cup tournament that amateur teams, if only for lack of regular training, were to all intents and purposes handicapped beyond help.

In order to encourage amateur sport, the Football Association determined to offer another cup, to be competed for by amateurs only. This was decided upon in 1893. At that time I was a member of the Football Association as the representative of the Middlesex Association. I was one of the committee who recommended the institution of the Amateur Cup Competition.

Whilst a member of the Council I acted as honorary secretary of the competition, and continued those duties to the end of my period of office.

This trophy has been the means of instilling ambition into many clubs and teams, chiefly in the far North and the South, but the tournament might have done still more good but for the persistent insinuations of a minority who seemed to think that the word "amateur" was solely applicable to the "Old Boys" clubs.

The middle and the working classes, it appeared, had no pretensions to be considered as sportsmen, and, in fact, had really no status at all, since they were not bona fide amateurs. Those who talked and wrote in this way did much harm to football and were manifestly unfair to the clubs and players competing and to the Amateur Cup Committee, who, however, had been appointed by what was described as a "professional" council! Did anyone ever hear such nonsense?

The Amateur Cup was first played for in 1893-94. And the Cup is still being played for without the "Old Boys," who allowed themselves to be prejudiced and led away by men of narrow vision. I regret that the Old Carthusians, the Old Malvernians, and the like did not remain in the lists. Seven or eight years after the foundation of the F.A. Amateur Cup, they would, perhaps, have gone over bodily to the Arthur Dunn Cup, but that is another story. The Old Carthusians were the first winners of both the Amateur Cup and the Dunn Cup. The membership of the "Old Boys" clubs is so considerable that they might have played for both these trophies.

Again let me remind those who are apt to forget, and inform those who have never known, that the Football Association revived their old amateur teams, went back to the days of amateurism and arranged international engagements for amateurs only. We were the first of the governing bodies in Great Britain to do so.

England played France at Paris on November 1, 1906, Ireland at Dublin, December 15, 1906, and Holland at The Hague, April 1, 1907. The Continental countries asked for matches, as they were anxious to learn the game. The F.A. decided to send amateur elevens, as this would be experience for our players and would encourage them. Besides, it would have been useless to choose professional teams, who would only have set up a standard that would have been disheartening to the comparative novices.

Now against France C.D. McIver (Old Foresters), P.H. Farnfield (New Crusaders), S.H. Day (Old Malvernians), and S.S. Harris (Old Westminsters) all played; against Ireland, T.S. Rowlandson (Old Carthusians), W.V. Timmis (Old Carthusians), K.R.G. Hunt (Corinthians, Trent College and Oxford U.) played; and against Holland, Rowlandson, Timmis, Hunt, G.N. Foster (Old Malvernians) and R.A. Young (Old Reptonians) played.

Any contemporary football annual will show that Old Boys, University men and Corinthians have been playing in these international games ever since, and most of us would like to know the difference between playing with the English amateurs against the teams of other nations, and playing against the same type of English amateurs in a Cup tie. When anyone begins to classify sportsmen, who are all equal on the turf and under it, it would seem that he sets himself a pretty task.

It is well not to forget that the amateurs of England and Ireland met in this new series of matches in 1906, that Wales became our opponent in 1908, and Scotland in 1926. There must have been a dearth of amateurs in Scotia.

Yet there came "the split." How did this arise? The county and the district associations affiliated to the F.A. were requested to make their rules conform to those of the parent body. This, of course, meant that professional clubs would become members of the provincial associations. Indeed, the Council of the F.A. passed a resolution that the time had arrived when the counties should accept as members the professional clubs within their area.

The London and Surrey Associations did not conform. The F.A. adhered to their resolution. Thereupon certain members of the Council, dissatisfied men, used this decision as a pretext to break away from the parent body and seize the opportunity of founding an association of their own.

There never should have been a split. That was my private considered opinion at the time, and it has been justified by the course of events, the return of several of the councillors who disagreed with the F.A. at the time, and the views, later in life, of Mr. H. Hughes-Onslow, who was the Honorary Secretary of the Amateur Football Association. Into this dispute, which lasted from 1907 until 1914, it is not necessary to enter, as unity has been restored on a basis mutually satisfactory.

The Amateur Football Association struggled bravely to carry on their own particular section of the game. Eventually the F.A. were approached by the A.F.A., who asked that they might be taken into membership with a definite constitution. This was, that their clubs should be mainly constituted of Public School Old Boys and business house clubs.

At first the A.F.A. could only take in clubs which were within their constitution. They are still working on those lines, but the F.A. have from time to time made concessions, agreeing to their acceptance of clubs other than those in the original constitution (twelve clubs per year), subject to those clubs continuing membership of their county associations.

Their total number of clubs is not to exceed 500, and their title has now been changed to that of The Amateur Football Alliance, which, like any other affiliated body, sends a representative to the Football Association.

To me these concessions indicate the interest that the F.A. take in amateur sport and their desire to encourage, rather than harm, those who play the game in life as well as on the field.

The general public have not the faintest idea that there are some 40,000 amateur clubs under the jurisdiction of the F.A., with about 750,000 amateur players—and this against 400 clubs who engage professionals.

There are only 5,000 registered professionals, and of these about one half are men who earn a living by following some trade or business and regard football as a hobby that brings a little more grist to the mill.

Obviously, the F.A. are a national association and not a "professional" association.

The general public, however, do not hear about the work done by the Association for the amateur and the smaller clubs. The newspapers devote their columns to those clubs with the largest number of adherents, camp-followers, mascot-bearers, or whatever term may be preferred.

The news concerns Aston Villa, not Beddington Corner, and Sunderland, not Crookhall Colliery Welfare. No editor cares much about Beddington and Crookhall, but he has an abiding interest in Aston Villa and Sunderland. The public have no idea of the work that is done by the F.A., because they have no opportunity of knowing.

Of course, if the Football Association punish a number of amateurs connected with clubs in Durham for receiving excessive expenses, say, for teas, the newspapers proclaim the infamy, or the incompetence, of the F.A. for their drastic treatment of trifling offences, while much greater ones are allowed to go without either suspensions or fines.

The F.A. had to take action in those Durham cases because of wholesale breaches of rules: payments in excess of expenses permissible, and the players never giving, nor the clubs demanding, receipts as required by the regulations.

Some of the suspensions were removed upon further evidence being produced, but no breaches of rules brought to the notice of the F.A. have ever been allowed to pass without punishment.

And after all, the Durham clubs were only treated in the same way as Metrogas and Barking Town. The governing bodies are very particular about all payments, whether to amateurs or professionals.

In recent years there has been a growing tendency to find situations for players—the amateur and the professional alike.

The professional, with the sanction of his club, wants some congenial occupation to supplement his salary as a footballer. He may wish to be a contributor to the newspapers, to be an inspector of the work of billstickers, to be a club doctor (for some players have medical degrees), or in any other business that his desire or ingenuity may suggest.

This, however, must involve duties apart from his football engagements. And I expect that any such matter would have to receive the approval of the League, who look after all domestic affairs of this kind.

Now the amateur is in a different class.

It has become a modern practice to find situations for men who are capable players. If this was done in Lancashire and other places over fifty years ago, I have no knowledge of the matter. The circumstances have changed.

Probably some football club placed a man in a cotton mill, and paid a salary for the work he did not do. His real work was on the field.

There has been the growth of welfare centres and clubs in connection with big business houses, factories, and workshops, and no doubt some competent artisans, "tradesmen" and clerks have been found employment by other clubs which are not off-shoots of great firms.

A university "Blue" may be appointed the secretary and manager of a Welfare Centre, with an Association team attached. A "Blue" may be chosen as a games-master for a good school. Probably each obtains the situation and the salary because of his athletic or football prowess, but he has the education and the capacity to do other work that might not be given to him unless he had these advantages.

The views which the F.A. have taken in any case brought to their notice, and their unswerving principle and practice, is that the man must not be given work other than his usual occupation. The labourer must not be appointed to a clerical position, and the carpenter must not be converted into a timekeeper for the factory. Skilled or unskilled in labour, the man must do his job.

This attitude reminds me of the old story of the vicar who advertised for a curate and added, in brackets, as a great qualification: (Fast Bowler Preferred). The line of demarcation between the amateur and the professional may appear to be very thin on occasion, but there is a line. The F.A. have always tried to act justly.

In 1933 the newspapers were asking why the Corinthians were favoured with exemption until the third round when they entered for the Cup, and why that exemption was eventually withdrawn. Any stick is good enough to beat a dog with, and any idle gossip has always been seized upon wherewith to attack the F.A.

The Corinthians never received a favour. There was no promise of exemption by Sir Charles Clegg, or anyone else, and therefore the promise was never revoked. No such "terms" were ever made.

It was part of the Corinthian creed not to enter for any competition. But the club became desirous of entering. They wished to be modern and test their strength.

In view of the fact that they do not play serious football until the season is well advanced, the club asked that they might be exempted until the first round of the Competition Proper.

The Corinthians, having preserved their love of the game, and being so popular with the public throughout the country, were accepted, and their request was granted; and very properly, too.

That this decision was perfectly correct there cannot be any doubt, for all the first-class professional teams were eager to be drawn against the Corinthians. They were a novelty, they could play a hard and enterprising game, and the crowd had a warm corner in their hearts for the "swells."

At first it seemed as if the Corinthians were almost on an equality with professionals; they proved themselves to be worthy opponents. But in recent seasons they have not maintained their splendid play, and therefore the exemption was withdrawn.

I am free to maintain they were properly exempted and also that the privilege was just as properly taken away.

The work of selecting clubs for exemption each year is referred to a sub-committee, who have to consider any clubs which have distinguished themselves in the Cup ties of the preceding season and the way the teams have acquitted themselves generally.

There are others to be considered, apart from the Corinthians. Justice has to be done to all clubs. Form, not favour, is the standard by which they are judged.

A club can only be placed as their play justifies. The Corinthians did not realize their own expectations; nor those of the committee by whom they were exempted. The Corinthians have been placed according to their merits. That is the inner history of the case.

Finally, in dealing with the relationship of the Association to amateur clubs, it does not seem quite apart from the subject to point out that by far the greater proportion of the revenue of the parent body comes from the matches played by professional players.

All these developments and experiments, to help on amateur football, have to be paid for, especially in their early stages.

Lots of things have been done for amateurs, for schools and universities, for county associations who have not a professional club in their area, for amateur clubs who wish to buy the freeholds of their grounds, and for all kinds of philanthropic and charitable institutions, apart from national appeals at times of great disasters, by means of the income that the Football Association derive from their international matches and from the percentages from Cup ties that have to be replayed. The professional clubs, as they are styled, and their players, help others and the community at large.

CHAPTER XIV

"CRIME" AND PUNISHMENT

THE six clubs of London that founded the Football Association just over seventy years ago had only one idea—to have one code of football for every man. In this they failed. Nevertheless, they banded themselves together and worked for what they conceived to be the ideal football. They had no precedents to guide them.

They brought in the first national governing body, the parent of all other societies and organizations that seek to rule some form of football. They were anxious to make their own particular form of recreation thoroughly popular. Some provincial clubs joined them, the most important being at Sheffield and Nottingham.

Even in those early days in the 'eighties, when there were only amateur clubs and players, the committee of this bold association introduced a rule to which I desire to call attention in view of the charge of autocratic and severe practices often brought against the F.A.

This rule, passed in 1884, reads: "The Committee … may call upon the clubs or individuals charged with offending against the rules, to prove to the satisfaction of the Committee that the offence has not been committed, and failing such satisfactory proof the clubs or individuals shall be adjudged guilty of the offence… The Committee shall have power to call upon any clubs or players to produce any books, letters or documents of any kind that the committee may desire."

The reader will notice that fifty years ago the F.A. did not assume that every man was innocent until he had been proved guilty. That was the ancient conception of justice. The F.A. called upon the club or the individual to prove that they had not done wrong, to "the satisfaction" of the committee. That was the law fifty years ago and it remains unchanged to this day.

Such rules, possibly thought autocratic by some people, are considered necessary in football. Whether that be of the amateur or professional kind is of no consequence, as they apply to all without exception. These rules existed before there was a man with the status of a professional.

It is necessary that I should emphasize such a matter as this, because I am about to tell the story of the downfall of Leeds City, the only club that the Association ever put out of the game for ever. "A severe sentence," the reader may say—but let us consider the facts.

When the European war broke out, the Football Association, after consultation with the War Office, suspended the international matches, the Association Cup tournament, closed the register for professional players, and ordered that no wages should be paid to anyone for playing football. No able-bodied man was to be allowed to stay in England and earn a livelihood as a professional footballer. The purpose was manifest.

Still, there were unofficial competitions for clubs in Lancashire, the Midlands and London. These were carried on by munition workers, soldiers on leave, and others who were allowed to remain at home. If any of them were professionals they just played where they liked, probably the nearest club to their work or camp. The condition was that these men were not to be paid wages.

The gross gates were handed to the League or other appointed officials. After the Entertainment Tax, a fixed percentage to charity, and a fixed levy for the maintenance of the League had been deducted, the clubs shared the net receipts, though I cannot remember upon what basis.

These matches were useful in many ways, especially as they interested spectators for an hour or two in times of grave anxiety and distress; they were really excellent alike for home workers and soldiers and sailors who were on leave.

In 1916-17 and 1917-18 Leeds City were the winners of the principal competition in the Midland Section. They managed to get some capable players, but there were allegations that these men were paid for their services. The Football Association appointed a Commission to enquire fully into the affairs of the club.

Under the rule that I have quoted, the books of the club were demanded and they were not forthcoming. The Commissioners were not satisfied, the authority of the F.A. had been disregarded.

The position was viewed seriously indeed by the Corporation of Leeds. The Lord Mayor sought an interview and pleaded for the club. All in vain; the books were never placed on the table. They were not to be obtained. The inference was that Leeds City had in a broad sense carried on as though no embargo had been placed upon their actions.

It was felt that improper payments had been made and that the books would prove it. The F.A. decided to suspend the club, the directors, and the officials for ever.

The governing body never makes any difference between persons whom they adjudge to have broken rules. The late Mr. Herbert Chapman, who was at that time the Secretary of the club, was considered to have been acting under the instructions of his directors, who were so stubbornly disobedient.

In one sense they were men enough to accept the suspicion of guilt fastened upon them and shield their helpers—the players.

When football was resumed under the auspices of the League in 1919-20, the players who were registered with that body returned to their respective clubs. Leeds City took their place in the Second Division, but in October, 1919, the club was suppressed, simply blotted out of the roll of members of the Association.

As there was no Leeds club, the Management Committee of the League appeared and took a hand in cleaning up the mess. Port Vale, who had only failed to secure election to this division by one vote, were offered the vacancy provided they would accept as their own record the results of the eight matches Leeds had played.

Still the League had another task. In 1919-20 they had a rule which said that "if any club is expelled, resigns, retires, or fails to gain re-election, the players whose names appear on the retain or transfer list of such clubs shall be held by the League, who shall fix the transfer fees of such players. The amount to be received shall belong to the League."

There was what some people have called an "auction" of the legitimate professionals in the service of Leeds City. This took place in one of the principal hotels of the city.

The last match that Leeds City played was at Wolverhampton against the Wanderers on October 4, 1919, and they won by 4–2. That day a sturdy north country lad, named Kirton, was playing at inside-right. The Aston Villa directors were watching, and when the "auction" took place this famous club secured him for a transfer fee of £250 and played him in the majority of their matches during the season.

Kirton appeared in the Final tie for the Cup at Chelsea, and is credited with the goal by which Aston Villa won the trophy in the extra half-hour against Huddersfield Town.

I believe that the ball was driven in by a kick from the corner flag, fell on Kirton's shoulders and touched Wilson, the centre half-back, as it flew into the net.

Kirton, who was originally a full-back, was the lucky man in that club disaster, although William Pease, who had never been signed, being really an amateur on trial, went to Northampton and thence to Middlesbro'. He played for England at outside right and was an adept whose centres were so often turned to account by Camsell.

Thus Leeds was deprived of its club, and the club lost their own players under the rules of the League. With that sequel the parent Association had nothing to do.

Whether Leeds City had paid their players I am not in a position to say, but the club was properly suppressed for an act of defiance to the ruling authority. No governing Association could tolerate such treatment. To do so would have been an encouragement to clubs to do just as they pleased.

Besides, it was treacherous to the Association, who had given an undertaking to the War Office that professionals should not be paid while there was a vital demand for men to serve their King and country in the gravest crisis through which we have ever passed.

Those who think that the F.A. were very severe have not a clear grasp of the facts.

There is another story about a neighbouring Yorkshire club during this trying period. I refer to Huddersfield Town. In the season of 1919-20, when Leeds City had become merely a memory, Huddersfield were threatened with dissolution for lack of funds. One of their founders, to whom Huddersfield were largely indebted, desired repayment, at least in part, of money advanced.

The club was in a desperate position, especially as this supporter, who had been so generous, conceived the idea of removing Huddersfield, lock, stock and barrel, to Leeds in order to play on the ground that Leeds City had no use for.

On the principle that threatened men live long, Huddersfield Town is still a big club. The people of Huddersfield did not like the idea of losing their club, even though most of them were adherents of the Rugby League.

They rallied to the club, and they were exhorted to do so by the captain of the team, Fred Bullock, originally an amateur full-back with Ilford. Bullock spoke up like a man who was not only a fine player, but had the existence of his club at heart.

He was earnestly supported by Mr. W.L. Hardcastle, who has represented the West Riding on the Council of the F.A. for eleven years. The players and the people of Huddersfield were roused to enthusiasm not only by Bullock's oratory but by the deeds of the team, who in this season were runners-up to Tottenham Hotspurs and gained promotion to the First Division.

Not only so, but they won their way into the Final for the Cup, and were only defeated by Kirton's goal. Mr. Rinder has publicly stated that the Villa never had a more thrilling and exhausting struggle in any Final than that against Huddersfield. He should know.

I have never known a club make a finer rally than did Huddersfield, and it is more than probable that this amazing effort would never have been made if there had not been this proposal to remove the club in a pantechnicon and unload it at the Elland Road ground in Leeds.

This Huddersfield team went one night to the Christmas pantomime at Leeds, where the story of *Aladdin* was being presented, with all the glitter of tinsel and theatrical craft for the umpteenth time on any stage. The yarn got about that the Huddersfield boys persuaded the "principal boy" to lend the team Aladdin's lamp.

They carried away the lamp, made it a mascot, took the art of the "property man" to every Cup tie, and simply worshipped it as if it were a shrine.

The "pot" was placed on the centre of the table in the dressing-room, the players walked round the table in a circle, and solemnly bowed. Such rites might have been performed by Red Indians on the trail or on an expedition.

They treasured this mascot, and as they won tie after tie, no doubt the players must have felt that there really was some magic about it. There was a time when they might have won the Cup. The goddess of Fortune forsook them when they did not seize the chances she gave them.

This campaign, with the lamp to light up their road, established Huddersfield so firmly that when Herbert Chapman was restored to the game he joined up with them. He and his helpers did great work, with what sequel we all know—that this Yorkshire club won the League championship in three consecutive years.

Of course, I am not quite so foolish as to believe that Aladdin's lamp and Chapman were mascots who did all this great work. Yet it is a strange world, and one can never tell what may have been the repercussions of the disaster to Leeds City.

These Yorkshire folk may quietly have resolved that their great county should not lose two League clubs. The "Tykes" simply swarmed the ground of Huddersfield when this great save-the-club movement began. These Northerners glory in a fight for life.

Perhaps the finest sequel to the Leeds City fall was that the gentleman who had the original notion of removing Huddersfield started another club on the old ground and called it Leeds United. Of course, there are others behind this new club, and Alderman Masser has a strong right hand in the secretary-manager, Richard

Ray, whom some will remember as a robust and far-seeing back.

When Leeds City was formed about 1905 he was their first captain. Now he has shown himself a shrewd judge of a footballer in the making, with the result that Leeds has had several seasons of First Division football and players of credit and renown.

Some people seem to have the strange idea that the Football Association meets with all the secrecy of the Star Chamber of centuries ago. There are those who hold that the F.A. love to punish and instil fear into directors and players; that they are a modern form of the Inquisition, with Sir Charles Clegg the Grand-Inquisitor.

If these feelings remain, I can assure those who suffer from such delusions that they are quite wrong. It is true that commissions are held in private. Only those who have business there, or are concerned with the proceedings, are allowed to be present.

Neither barristers nor solicitors can be employed to plead in the ordinary way. A barrister or a solicitor can represent a club, a competition or an association if he be either the chairman or secretary of any one of these bodies. Even then he does so as an official, not as a member of the legal profession.

The football community has to trust the Football Association. The sound way this body has dispensed justice ever since I can remember is proved by the fact that the Association have never lost an action brought against them in the law courts.

Sir Charles Clegg, as I have already stated, is a solicitor, and has been accustomed to examine and cross-examine witnesses and those who make statements. When a decision has to be made, or a finding pronounced and published, Sir Charles Clegg has always acted on one plan. Over and over again he has said: "Let us never do anything that we cannot justify, if need be, in a court of law. We are the guardians of the game, but our zeal as trustees must not over-ride our sense of justice and our responsibility to the public. We must always do our duty without fear or favour and retain the confidence of the public."

That is the spirit in which all the inquiries and commissions have been conducted, and the basis of all the findings.

CHAPTER XV

THE GLAMOUR OF "THE CUP"

THE story of the Association Cup is very remarkable. Were there a stadium twice the size of the spacious enclosure at Wembley, the public would fill it, as the great sporting carnival of April arrived. The world always wants to know the winner of the Derby and the victorious team in the Final Tie for what is generally called the English Cup.

Such a title is not correct, because the first rule of the tournament reads: "The Cup shall be called 'The Football Association Challenge Cup." But everyday folk have preferred "The English Cup"—for short.

The progress of the popularity of the game can be traced by the records of the Final Tie, for this match has been an accurate register of public interest.

The first Final was played on March 16, 1872, and *Bell's Life*, the famous sporting newspaper of that era, made the statement that there were few spectators at Kennington Oval, "the reason being possibly that an admission fee of 1s. was charged."

That may be so, but we also read: "That the Association code can ever rival the Rugby Union game in public estimation can hardly be hoped for by its most sanguine admirers"

In the following season the Final Tie was played on March 29, 1873, at Lillie Bridge ground, now occupied by railway lines at West Brompton. We are told that the kick-off was fixed for 11 a.m., in order to enable players and their friends to see the University Boat Race, but before the ball was set in motion the clock indicated half-past that hour. There is no mention of any crowd of sightseers.

The Boat Race was rowed on the same day as the Final was decided in 1877, 1888 and 1889. That they were so near to being on the same day in previous years was because the teams and their supporters desired to see the race while "up for the Cup."

In 1874 there were "upwards of 2,000 spectators," but in 1875 only half that number, the decline being attributed to a cold north-east wind. The struggle to gain adherents who would face any wind or weather was long and trying. Not until 1878 can I find the mention of 3,000 spectators.

The game "arrived" slowly, for in 1880 the attendance, 5,000, was described as the "largest." Mark the steady progress: in 1881, 5,000 people; in 1882, 6,000; in 1883, 10,000—"the largest crowd ever seen."

The provinces were asserting themselves. The "hordes of the North," the "thousands of flat caps" and other strange descriptions, were applied to the "countrymen" who travelled to London each spring for the match.

From 1874 to 1892 each Final Tie was decided at the Oval, but in the interests of the summer game the Surrey Cricket Club then decided to discontinue the use of the ground for the playing of football.

In 1893 the Final Tie was taken to the ground of the Manchester Athletic Club, at Fallowfield. Why? Because this was the only enclosure big enough to accommodate the ever-increasing crowd. The area of the ground was ample, but there was so little stand accommodation that the arrangements proved quite inadequate, and a complete fiasco was only narrowly averted.

In 1894 the match was allotted to the football arena of the Everton Club; but it was becoming palpable that the Final Tie required a larger ground than any in existence.

Then came a suggestion that the match should be played in the grounds of the Crystal Palace, on the bed of an artificial lake that had been drained and was richly covered with grass and surrounded by an amphitheatre clothed with turf.

There was ample space, but again very poor stand

accommodation.

I was, as a member of the Council, placed on the sub-committee of the Football Association appointed to confer with the Crystal Palace authorities. There was nowhere else to go, or so suitable, as the arena was not used by any club, was absolutely neutral, and was so situated that a massed multitude on the lawn and on the rising ground behind could obtain a view of the game.

Terms were mutually settled, the Football Association to take 90 per cent. of the gross gate. The first match at Sydenham, between Aston Villa and West Bromwich Albion, in 1895, attracted between 42,000 and 43,000 people, a great assembly at that time—which, be it remembered, was only ten years after the introduction of professionalism.

The register of public approval of our game was continually rising. And there was never a serious check. The twenty Final Ties at the Crystal Palace had an average attendance of over 73,000 people.

On three occasions the inflowing tide mounted to six figures, for in 1901, when Tottenham Hotspur and Sheffield United met, the attendance was 110,820; in 1905, with Aston Villa and Newcastle in opposition, 101,117; and in 1913, when Aston Villa and Sunderland were also battling for the League championship, 120,081.

Just when such figures as these were compelling the Association to think about the future, the Great War broke out. There was no Final Tie between 1915 and 1920.

When the Cup was again offered for competition, the Chelsea Club's ground was the rendezvous. This was Hobson's choice. Neither London nor the provinces had a ground so large and fully equipped as we desired. With peace restored there was a revival and a sudden expansion of the sporting spirit.

There were three Finals at Chelsea. The first, Aston Villa and Huddersfield, brought to the exchequer £9,772 10s.; the second, Tottenham and Wolverhampton, £13,414 4s. 6d.; and the third, Huddersfield and Preston, £10,551 6s. 6d. The average attendance was reduced to 58,600, but the increased prices of admission and stands brought a larger revenue.

The housing of the Final Tie became a difficult problem. The founders of the Cup never anticipated, could never have hoped for, such vast assemblies and such receipts.

Should the Football Association acquire a large estate and make a Hampden Park in London? It was felt that such a move would meet with the disapproval of the public, would centralize all big matches in London, and that its occasional use would not justify the parent body in embarking upon such an expensive enterprise, with its additional cost of maintenance.

The Crystal Palace again came under consideration, and the outlay of a large sum to adapt that ground to modern needs was under discussion when an imperial exhibition was projected on a site at Wembley.

There was a suggestion that the Football Association should become interested in a proposal to build a great stadium at Wembley Park.

This was brought to my notice in the spring of 1921, when Major E.A. Belcher, C.B.E., the assistant general manager of the company which had been formed to undertake the preliminary negotiations in connection with the holding of a British Empire Exhibition in 1923, called upon me.

Vaguely I recalled Wembley Park. I associated it with the name of Sir Edward Watkin and a scheme to build a tower to compare favourably with the Eiffel Tower at Paris. I thought the best thing to do was to visit the Park and meet the officials of the Exhibition.

The Park was being used as a golf course, and as we ascended the hill on which the stadium now stands, I was astonished to see the foundations of the tower which it was proposed at one time to erect. This was known for ever so long as "Watkin's Folly."

The lift shaft of this tower is buried beneath the royal entrance to the present stadium, and it gave the engineers some trouble when the ground was being cleared.

I was much impressed when the complete scheme was unfolded by Major Belcher and reported to what was called the Ground Committee, who, accompanied by myself, visited

Wembley on May 8, 1921, and had an interview with Major Belcher. The suitability of the site and the construction of a ground adequate for the Final Tie were considered.

A few days afterwards the Finance Committee met Major Belcher and representatives of the Ministry of Transport, the Metropolitan Railway and the Great Central Railway. At the end of May, Sir Charles Clegg had completed a draft agreement from notes submitted to him, and the agreement with the Exhibition authorities was soon concluded.

In this way the Football Association not only provided for a stadium to be built, but also made it possible for the British Empire Exhibition to be proceeded with and eventually opened.

Need I say that this stadium is an all-British creation in every way. It was built at a cost of £300,000 in twelve months, and is the largest amphitheatre—ancient or modern—in the world. It was designed to accommodate 125,000 people, but, for purposes of safety, comfort and a perfect view, the space has been rearranged for 92,000 people or thereabouts.

The agreement as originally drawn was to be in force for twenty-one years, the Football Association, the competing clubs and the Stadium each taking one-fourth of the receipts, the Stadium to pay all expenses of upkeep and control of the match.

The first Final Tie at this stadium was played on April 29, 1923, four days after the workmen had completed their task, in what was then declared to be a record time for an erection of this magnitude.

As most people who are interested in football will recall, the match was between Bolton Wanderers and West Ham United, and His Majesty King George V. had graciously promised to attend, as he did. The weather, the opening of the stadium, the presence of a London club, and the visit of the King combined to draw a tremendous concourse of sightseers.

The official figures of the attendance were 126,047. These people passed through the turnstiles, but no one can estimate the numbers who avoided the turnstiles, gained admission in all manner of ways, and appropriated seats and places that they were not entitled to.

Some said that there were 250,000 people in the ground, but this may be taken as an exaggeration. It must suffice to say that not only was all accommodation for visitors occupied, but the playing arena was covered with thousands who had come to see the match, which they themselves were preventing from being started at the appointed hour.

Seeing the ground in this state of confusion I went to the entrance for royalty. This was entirely open. To erect gates had not been considered necessary. When His Majesty arrived, I said to him:

"I fear, sir, that the match may not be played. The crowd has broken in. The playing-ground is covered with people."

As His Majesty caught a glimpse of the massed crowd at the end of the tunnel leading to the Royal Box he said: "Whose fault is that?" I felt that I could only bow and smile.

What could I do or say? The King, seeing the predicament, simply said: "What do you want me to do?" I replied: "If Your Majesty will kindly go into the Royal Box we will see what we can do to clear the ground."

As soon as King George was seen there, every face was turned towards him. The great assembly remained silent and still while the bands played the National Anthem. I felt that there was a possibility of order.

I murmured to myself: "The King will save the situation." The police made an effort to clear the ground. The teams were brought out. The policeman on the white horse rode about to press the people back.

All to no effect. His Majesty waited. The obvious conclusion was that the match could not be played. The spectators thronged the ground. They wandered about aimlessly.

Then, as if by the magic of telepathy, I saw the eyes of thousands of trespassers directed towards the Royal Box where His Majesty was standing, watching what must have been a very interesting and wonderful scene.

What is going to happen? must have been the question passing through his mind, as with others who had some responsibility.

Then, all at once, the people grasped their opportunity of seeing their King at closer quarters. Probably many had never seen him before and might never see him again.

They surged in the direction of the Royal Box. They could not turn back. They passed within a few yards of His Majesty. Each person having had his own private "close-up," as moderns say, of his Sovereign Lord, The King, felt perfectly satisfied, and strolled on through the tunnel which led from the stadium to the exhibition ground.

Tens of thousands passed by in this way, the playing area was gradually cleared and those who had seen their King were gratified and satisfied.

The probability is that if the wait could have been extended for another quarter of an hour the whole of the ring would have been free from intruders and the game played under normal conditions, whereas there were people close up to all the boundary lines. This is the story of the match as it is impressed on my memory.

The crowd, under the spell of the King's gaze, was drawn in his direction and solved the difficulty. When the King came to one of the Finals some years later I ventured to remind him of the opening of the stadium, and added: "Had you not been here, sir, the match would never have been played."

His Majesty, with a spice of fervour, answered, "I know it. I know it would not have been played."

And let us never forget that the King waited three-quarters of an hour for the kick-off, whatever may have been the entries upon the pages of his private diary and his inmost desire.

Our King, as the reigning monarch, watched the Final Tie for the first time in 1914, and stayed to present the trophy and the medals to Burnley and Liverpool. Whenever it has been possible for His Majesty to come among his people and share their interest in our manly sport at this annual national festival, he has done so.

As the patron of the Football Association he has rendered great service to our game, but never more so than at the opening of the Wembley Stadium, for the postponement of that Final would have been little short of a disaster.

The sequel was an inquiry by the Home Office into the management of crowds on all occasions such as this, and finally the adoption by the Football Association of an all-ticket Final.

Since 1923 no money has been taken at turnstiles on this occasion. Every person must purchase his ticket in advance, and no more are sold than the Stadium will comfortably accommodate. This precaution was not popular when introduced, but the wisdom of the change has been proved and appreciated.

There is no more orderly spectacle in the realm of sport than the Final Tie. Some have described it as a football ceremony; but better that than a fiasco.

For the first ten years in which this match was played there were never more spectators than an ordinary gathering for a Third Division League match of these days, whereas now there are always about 93,000 people, who include visitors from many parts of the Empire and from foreign countries.

There is no evidence of popularity so strong as that of the Box Office, and the fact that the leading newspapers of the world furnish their readers with reports of the event.

And all this is due to the decision of seven men who met in the office of a London newspaper on a July day in 1871 and unanimously resolved, "That it is desirable that a challenge Cup should be established in connection with the Association, for which all clubs belonging to the Association should be invited to compete." And that at a time when there was not any money to buy a trophy!

The clubs were asked for donations to buy a modest trophy. That is in conformity with the wording of the resolution "that a challenge Cup should be established."

The seven men who laid the foundation of this knock-out tournament of thrilling games were Charles Alcock, my immediate predecessor as secretary of the F.A., Captain Francis Marindin (as he was then called), M.P. Betts, who scored the first goal in any Final Tie, and the only one, when playing in the name of A.H. Chequer (a Harrow Chequer), A. Stair, of Upton Park (the honorary treasurer of the F.A.), D. Allport, of the Crystal Palace club and the Wanderers, J.H. Giffard, of the Civil Service, and C.W. Stephenson, of Westminster School. All honour to these seven men who built better than they knew.

It is recorded in the Minute Book that the majority of the clubs "signified their intention of competing." The captains of the clubs were called together and the competition was organized in October, 1871.

In this quiet way the most exciting of all football tournaments was framed. For ten seasons there was a struggle, but when interest spread and a provincial club, the Blackburn Rovers, first made an appearance in the Final Tie, it became clear that a national football festival day was being established.

It is so long ago that I cannot precisely recall the first Final I ever saw. That was a red-letter day, but no one thought so at that time.

I used to go regularly to the Kennington Oval, and my earliest recollection is that the Surrey cricket club had small movable stands that we described as "flowerpot stands." People were eager to lie down on the grass between these temporary stands and the touch line.

Members of the ground committee were in the habit of collecting half-a-crown from each person in this enclosure. Tom Gunning, of the London Association, and one of the vice-presidents of the F.A., and myself used to fill our pockets with half-crowns.

There were others, and we all went into the pavilion and poured our treasure on the tables to those who were appointed to receive the money. How primitive!

The idea makes me laugh when I think of the days when men like Lord Rosebery, Mr. Arthur Balfour, Lord Alverstone, and the Rt. Hon. Alfred Lyttelton would come to the match and present the Cup and medals to the players.

It was my duty to invite such notabilities and the F.A. never had a refusal. The Final was most interesting to all the great men. Is it any wonder that sport and fashion have combined to draw multitudes on these historic occasions?

CHAPTER XVI

FAMOUS FINALS OF THE PAST

THE annals of the Association Cup convey more than the development of popular interest in this form of football. They provide a fascinating story of the changes that have occurred in the game.

As I look at the list of winners of the Cup in the official handbook that the Council of the F.A. issues at the beginning of each season, I think that the record shows how the Old Boys of the big Public Schools provided the material for the strong amateur teams from 1872 to 1883, what a force the Lancashire clubs became from 1884 to 1893, how the Midland counties asserted themselves from 1894 to 1905, the strong grip that the Northerners obtained from 1906 to 1915, and the awakening of the Southern professional clubs from 1920 to 1930.

No competition has had more effect on the game than the Cup, for this knock-out tournament gradually created such an overwhelming passion for success that professionalism was introduced.

I am not to be tempted into an argument concerning the effects of paying men for playing football.

Such a subject has many phases, but professional football has set a high technical standard, and has provided a splendid open-air entertainment for millions of people.

The spectacular side of the game is undoubtedly a national asset and has caused thousands of clubs to spring into existence, with hundreds of thousands of young men always striving to play well.

With professionals in their teams, clubs felt the need of a regular series of matches that Cup-ties on the knock-out principle could never supply.

I have been informed that in the minute book of 1883–84, kept by the West Bromwich Albion club, there is a memorandum that the committee decided not to issue a list of fixtures, as "the playing off of Cup-ties makes it impossible to present a reliable list; in fact, it is simply a question of making an arrangement and then cancelling it." That was the effect of Cup-ties.

The Football League was therefore invented primarily to draw up a permanent programme for the season, and the Association Cup-ties were so rearranged as to give clubs the opportunity of fulfilling fixtures to provide a reliable revenue. This was a need that professionalism created.

Hence, directly and indirectly, the foundation of the Cup altered the football plan. Nevertheless, the Cup-ties have for many reasons retained their attractiveness, and the climax of the season is the Final Tie for the trophy in April.

This, as I have already shown, has become the most appealing and interesting football match in all the world. Neither the passing of the years, nor the radical changes caused by grouping clubs and in styles of play, necessitated by new laws of the game, has adversely affected this festival or reduced its magnetic power upon both the classes and the masses.

I was not quite fourteen years old when the first Final Tie was played, but in the accounts of the newspapers in 1872 I read, even in those days of unsullied amateurism, that the Royal Engineers were "the favourites" when they met the Wanderers, who were the Corinthians of that period. Odds of seven to four were laid on the Engineers. And this before professionalism was dreamed of!

Let us not forget that in this era betting on the University Boat Race was always quoted in the public prints. Nevertheless, I was surprised to see that there had been odds quoted on the first Final—even though it may be contended that this was due to the vogue of gambling on almost any event.

For all that, the Football Association have always been

opposed to any form of gambling.

The Royal Engineers were defeated by 1–0, but there is this to be said on their behalf, that Lieutenant Creswell broke his collar-bone ten minutes from the kick-off. He did not retire.

One newspaper states that "he maintained his post to the finish of the game." Another chronicler, Major-General Sir Richard M. Ruck, in a very interesting reminiscent article in *The Royal Engineers' Journal*, records that Creswell "very pluckily played on to the end of the match."

Perhaps men were tougher over sixty years ago than now, for I can hardly imagine any player, under such circumstances, enduring to the end in these days.

Still, I remember that in the first Final Tie decided at the Crystal Palace in 1895, the centre half-back of West Bromwich Albion, "Tom" Higgins, had his head cut open.

This was a nasty gash. He went to the dressing room, had the wound attended to and dressed. He returned wearing a wide bandage round his head, and Colonel North, the millionaire, presented him with a five-pound note as an expression of his admiration.

But serious injuries in the Final have been very rare.

In those amateur days the game was by no means gentle. That famous sportsman, C.J. Ottaway, playing for the Old Etonians against the Engineers, "received such a severe kick on the ankle that he had to be carried off"—an accident which, we are told, "made the game equal, allowing for the wind." This, by way of comment, must bring a smile.

An extra half hour had to be played in spite of Ottaway's accident. Of course he could not take part in either the extra time or the replay, three days afterwards.

When the Wanderers won for the third year in succession, in 1878, it is stated that their goalkeeper, J. Kirkpatrick, had his arm broken during a vigorous attack by the Engineers, but "he saved the goal and pluckily stuck to his post to the end."

I remember well the match of 1883, when Blackburn Olympic, after extra time, defeated the Old Etonians. It should, however, be noted that when the game was "one all," Arthur T.B. Dunn was hurt and retired.

When the Old Etonians were becoming tired, the two centre-forwards, R.H. Macaulay and H.C. Goodhart, were injured.

Nevertheless, the Old Etonians did not demur to extra time; but they were beaten more by the physical fitness of the Olympic than any other factor.

In presenting the Cup, Major Marindin said that the Olympic could fairly claim to be the champions of the season, and he hoped their success would encourage other young clubs.

As it happened, the triumph of the working classes was so complete, in its effects, that the Old Boys have never since been seen in the Final Tie.

These men from the public schools played, as I have shown, with indomitable pluck and great skill as individualists.

In the Old Etonian eleven for this Final there were six international players in J.F.P. Rawlinson (afterwards counsel for the F.A.), P.J. de Paravicini, Hon. A.F. Kinnaird (afterwards President of the F.A.), R.H. Macaulay, H.C. Goodhart, and A.T.B. Dunn.

Rawlinson, cool and sure, as goalkeeper, Paravicini, a speedy back using either foot splendidly, and Arthur Dunn, a fast forward who dribbled well and centred accurately, would have held their own had they played in this day.

The late Arthur Dunn, commemorated for all time by the Dunn Cup, captained England against Scotland, as the left back, at Glasgow in 1892, nine years later.

He, the only amateur in the eleven, played a great part in the decisive victory of the "old crocks," as they were called, over the Scots. The combination of the English forwards was wonderful.

I could choose a splendid team from the Finalists of the Old Boys' period.

By the way, I feel that I must call attention to the formation of the Royal Engineers in 1875, as they played a goal-keeper, a three-quarter back, two half-backs, and seven forwards, two on each wing, and three centre-forwards.

As they were placed they had virtually three backs, and one

of them was named Lieut. Sim, who has been described as the first player who made a practice of heading the ball—a development that has made one or two modern backs as valuable as a second goalkeeper.

All honour to these pioneers who first aroused interest in the Final Tie. I am not quite sure, though, whether the Blackburn Olympic should have had the opportunity of being the first provincial team to win the Cup and take it North.

In 1882, the Blackburn Rovers, the first provincial eleven to appear in this match, had also to meet the Old Etonians, who won by 1–0, owing to Dunn's speed in a breakaway and his exact pass to W.J. Anderson on the opposite wing.

The late John Lewis, who was a member of the Council for so many years, never complained about the absence of D.H. Greenwood, a fine back, or an accident to one of the Rovers' forwards, but he did say that the match was lost when C.W. Alcock, the secretary of the FA., wrote to the Rovers and pointed out the similarity of the colours of the clubs.

The Etonians wore light-blue and white harlequin shirts. As the Rovers were usually attired in similar jerseys, the first thing they did on reaching London was to visit a big warehouse and take their own outfitter.

The Rovers played in black and white stripes and "Honest John" clapped his hands in his most emphatic manner as he said: "This lost us the match?" He had no doubt in his own mind.

Still, Blackburn Rovers should have been satisfied with victories in 1884, 1885 and 1886. Their struggles with Queen's Park are historic.

The Queen's did not agree with some of the decisions of the referee, but even so the Rovers proved the more brilliant in forward manœuvres.

For the first time in any Final Tie the Rovers, in 1885, played three half-backs, and a great three they were—George Howarth, Hugh McIntyre and James Forrest—all of international rank.

When the Blackburn Rovers won in three successive years it was pointed out by Major Marindin that they had equalled the run of the Wanderers, but James Brown, the captain and dashing centre-forward, replied that football was in its infancy in the days of the Wanderers!

I am aware that Aston Villa and West Bromwich Albion earned much renown in this period, from 1884 to 1893, but do not forget that in the ten Finals of these years Lancashire was represented on eight occasions and provided six winners—Blackburn Rovers five times and Preston North End.

The Rovers excelled in Cup Finals. They twice conquered Queen's Park, who virtually represented Scotland at that time.

They overcame West Bromwich Albion, then a purely English eleven developing into one of the most sparkling teams ever seen. In fact, I doubt whether there was ever such a thrilling set of local players in any club as that of the Albion in 1886, 1887 and 1888. Their doughty deeds can never be forgotten by those who saw them.

When the Blackburn Rovers and the Albion had drawn at the expiration of time in 1886, the Staffordshire lads volunteered to play extra time, but the Rovers refused.

The replay was at Derby in mid-week, after a snowstorm, and the Rovers won largely through "Jimmy" Brown, who was a superb centre to watch, because of his daring thrustfulness and control in dribbling. His goal, which put the issue beyond doubt, was a masterpiece of dribbling, swerving and, finally, shooting.

"Jimmy" Brown in his heyday was as popular as any centre ever known. He was a Blackburn lad, a solicitor's clerk, with only a modest physique: he stood 5 ft. 5½ in. and I should say he was not ten stone in weight—these details, so universal now, were not then common newspaper property.

His attacks down the centre typified his personality, for he was fearless and fair, and always merry and bright.

In the fourth season after vanquishing the "Throstles," as the West Bromwich men were called, after the songsters of South Staffordshire, the Rovers simply extinguished Sheffield Wednesday by the then unprecedented score of 6–1 in their fifth appearance in the Final.

Three of the goals were shot by William Townley, an outside-left, who was, I believe, a schoolmaster.

All sorts of fables were told to account for the downfall of Wednesday.

Sheffield was shocked, but most of their local team were suffering from football injuries, the forward line had to be rearranged and the half-backs were so busy in defence that they could render little assistance to the Wednesday vanguard.

And yet Haydn Morley, the Derby gentleman who was the right-back, was carried off the Oval by enthusiasts as a tribute to his sportsmanship and skill.

The next year Blackburn Rovers ran away with the trophy when Notts County were hoping to repeat the League victory they had gained over the Rovers, who had been playing so well during their first season on what is now called Ewood Park.

Notts had beaten the Rovers by 7–1, and Dr. Morley said that the latter played like old women in clogs would have done.

On a windy March day, at the Oval, the Rovers virtually decided their sixth Final in the first half, as they scored three times, and Notts County, without two of their safest defenders, were never able to rally.

Does the reader know any club with a more handsome record than Blackburn Rovers in their six Finals, five of which they won, with a goal average of 15–4?

The answer from some will be "Yes." The Wanderers of the 'seventies, who were never defeated in five Finals, won by an aggregate of 11–1.

All honour be rendered to the Wanderers, but it should be remembered that Blackburn Rovers played in three Finals in the amateur era, and three more after professionalism had been sanctioned; the conditions changed and teams became even more solid and balanced than in these days when there are nearly four times as many League clubs seeking players.

It is an illuminating fact that Blackburn Rovers had to wait for 37 years before they had the opportunity of registering their sixth victory when they routed Huddersfield Town, then second in the

League Championship, while the Lancashire club was smiling with safety, and relieved of all anxieties, except a fervent wish to equal the record of six Cup victories by Aston Villa.

I do not exaggerate when I say that the Rovers just blotted out Huddersfield. I have seldom seen a wing half-back so completely check-mate an international Scottish raider like A. Jackson, as did A.F. Campbell in this match.

That day Campbell was a revelation. The old passion of the Rovers had, in some mysterious way, been preserved. This family heirloom was the mascot. What the Rovers had done they could do again.

From my experience of Final Ties I have come to the conclusion that force of personality is far more potent than technical skill.

There was a more accomplished team than Blackburn Rovers in this period from 1884 to 1893, and yet only once could they win the Cup.

I refer, as may readily be guessed, to Preston North End, who, in my judgment, were the best team of all time—ancient or modern.

I cannot recall the Wanderers, although I saw them and knew all about them at that time. Still, there have been great teams at Preston, at Sunderland, at Aston with the Villa, at West Bromwich, at Blackburn, at Newcastle, and I might add at London, the Arsenal in particular, since 1929.

Yet, only the Rovers, the Villa and the Albion have lived up to the colloquial description of being "great Cup fighters."

I have written about the mysterious family heirloom. It is strange how tradition lives on and on in a club once it becomes famous for success of one kind.

Why should the Blackburn Rovers and Aston Villa have each become the guardians of the Cup six times?

Why should West Bromwich, so near to Aston Villa and so attractive to ambitious players, have earned such a reputation for Cup conquest?

Why should Sunderland possess such a sad record in the

Cup?

To me there is only one explanation. The club with a series of victories in Cup Finals has been fortunate in possessing men who have the "big match" temperament, who play better than their best when the need is supreme; who are daring, dauntless and determined; and who combine such attributes with just sufficient skill to overcome adversaries more talented in technical skill.

It is the personal force of character that turns the scale and causes results that are described as surprises.

Preston North End have done what no other club has done, or probably ever will do.

This greatest feat in all football stands to the immortal credit of Preston—the winning of the League Championship without loss of a match and the winning of the Association Cup without loss of a goal in the whole competition.

Preston have never had their equals.

Their players from 1885–86 to 1888–89 could do all that the ultra-moderns can do, and do it better, with more accuracy and fewer mistakes.

In each position every man was a master. They had physique, science, touch and perfect understanding.

And yet in 1887 West Bromwich Albion could beat Preston in a semi-final tie; and in 1888 the "Throstles" could conquer the proud pets of Preston in the Final Tie at Kennington.

Once only could Preston win this Cup, and that in 1889, when their half-backs defied criticism and their forwards were able to win as they liked and then play to please the "gallery" by their finesse.

And yet with all their skill, when they could beat the Blackburn Rovers in four matches out of every six, the East Lancashire lads were immeasurably superior when force of personality was called for.

CHAPTER XVII

GREAT CUP-TIE TEAMS

JUST as Blackburn Rovers were the dominating club in the period from 1884 to 1893, so do Aston Villa stand out as the great club of the seasons from 1894 to 1905. This era of triumph for the Midlands was ushered in by the win of Wolverhampton Wanderers over Everton by a shot from "Harry" Allen, the centre half-back, who had just previously tried to kill a policeman with one of his whiz-bang drives at the goal.

When West Bromwich and Wolverhampton had won the silver bauble, with teams of English lads, they stood on a level with Aston Villa, who carried off the trophy in the Jubilee year of Queen Victoria's reign, and that with a team which Mr. F.W. Rinder declared had not cost a penny!

Miracles were occasionally seen in those days, but there were then many players for few clubs, whereas now there are many clubs for few players of unquestioned ability.

Aston Villa were very ambitious. They still are.

Yet it was in this period that the Midlands were supreme, for Aston Villa gained three more victories in the Final Tie, and twice the Cup went to the ancient city of Nottingham, where the game had been played by two clubs, Notts County and Nottingham Forest, since the early years of the Victorian 'sixties.

The County began with a number of bankers and lawyers as chasers of our big ball, and aimed at being a county eleven, while the Foresters were a town team.

Both these clubs have had many fine footballers, and we greybeards can recall the time when Notts County consisted mostly of English international players connected with the district. Yet they never quite realized expectations.

Their poor performance against Blackburn Rovers in 1891 was forgotten in 1894 when Notts won the Cup by defeating Bolton Wanderers 4–1 at Everton. This was a wholly professional team and was the first club in the Second Division of the League to master a member of the higher division in one of these historic matches.

While Bolton Wanderers were not by any means thoroughly fit, there is no doubt to my mind that for about six weeks Notts County had the best set of players in the land; captained by David Calderhead, a keen centre half-back who played hard-tackling, clever football.

Notts had a fine centre in James Logan, whose dribbling and shooting on the eventful day would have outwitted the strongest teams. Like Townley, of Blackburn, four years earlier, in 1890, Logan scored three consecutive goals, and heaven only knows how many more would have been obtained if Bolton had not, at that time, had one of the finest defences ever seen, with J.W. Sutcliffe in goal, and he "covered" by such backs as John Somerville and Dai Jones.

Let me call to the mind of readers that Sutcliffe was a first-class Rugby international three-quarter who also kept goal for England against our British neighbours. It is doubtful if there was ever a brilliant custodian quite so safe.

With Dai Jones, who often played for Wales, and Somerville, a Scotsman almost as reliable, the Notts men confronted one of the soundest defences in history, and I am not forgetting W.R. Moon and the brothers Walters, and Doig ("Ned" he was called) with McCombie and James Watson of Sunderland.

Each of these defences was of international rank, and the Bolton Wanderers' men deserved as much distinction, but they represented different countries, and Somerville did not catch the eyes of the selectors. Still, he was a shrewd, neat, sound and fair player.

Nottingham Forest had their day in 1898 at the Crystal

Palace, when they were far too skilful and well balanced for Derby County. Even so, this Final was rather disappointing, for neither team produced its best football.

Both these old clubs had waited long for the Cup they had been expected to carry off teens of years before they actually did so.

When the Forest and the County were at their zenith and relied on native sportsmen, a combination of their two elevens would, I think, have beaten a native team from any city or town in England.

Between the triumphs of the Nottingham clubs, Aston Villa won twice. There is not much to be said about their success over West Bromwich Albion, even though this game decided a unique rubber in Finals, for no other neighbouring rivals have thrice met on these momentous occasions.

I should say that never was a Final decided so quickly as this event in 1895, for the Villa scored the only goal before many people had taken their positions or their seats.

This first Final at the Crystal Palace ran its full 90 minutes, according to law, but in less than a minute from the kick-off that tear-away outside-right, Athersmith, made a centre that enabled R. Chatt to shoot.

The ball looked like entering the net, but was deflected to John Devey, who beat Reader, the keeper of the goal.

I give these details as related by Mr. Rinder, the chairman of the Villa for so many years, as there has been much argument about the point and who really placed the ball into the net.

Possibly the Albion were unfortunate, but on the whole it was the general impression that Aston Villa were rather the better eleven, although William Bassett, who afterwards became chairman of his club and a member of the Council of the F.A., with his partner, "Roddy" McLeod, formed a great wing. It is doubtful if Bassett ever had such an unselfish helpmate.

The next appearance of Aston Villa at the Crystal Palace was in 1897. Their opponents were Everton, and this encounter might well be described as the Diamond Jubilee Final, for at that time the critics agreed that this was the finest match ever played in the series.

Even to this day veterans declare that for quality and sportsmanship the conflict has never been equalled.

Fifteen of the players were either international men at that time, or became so, and the Villa had only a slight advantage reckoning on this basis. As there was only a goal between them, perhaps the odd international won the match, for G.F. Wheldon was responsible for two of them.

Many a time we have had long to wait for the first goal in the Final, but on this occasion all the five goals were scored within 35 minutes of the kick-off.

Campbell and Wheldon were responsible for the Villa's three, and John Bell and R.H. Boyle, the right half-back, for Everton's pair.

Everton toiled throughout that second half to re-establish equality and then hope for the best. It seemed as if every man could never have played so well in his career.

The previous Saturday John Bell had assisted Scotland against England, at the Crystal Palace, in the same position—outside-right. This chip of Dumbarton's rock took his bearings that day. He was quite at home on this big arena.

By his raids, so ingenious in evasion and so sure in centring, he did all that a man could do to save this match. Yet all was in vain.

On Everton's left there were Edgar Chadwick and Milward, than whom I never saw a better wing. Chadwick, with the footwork of a juggler in his control of the ball, and perfect in his pass and position play, was probably as great a master as "Nuts" Cobbold, whose dribbling has become legendary.

Milward was very dangerous, being strong, swift and a shot. He used to middle the ball so well. And Everton had a brilliant set of half-backs.

Yet Aston Villa won well, and I remember that the late Lord Rosebery, who presented the prizes, as we said at school, described the match as an Olympian struggle that he would never forget.

Well might he say so, for in the last twenty minutes Everton maintained a grand attack, but could not overcome such backs as Howard Spencer and Albert Evans, who had in front of them John Reynolds, James Cowan and James Crabtree.

Nor can I close this tribute to Aston Villa without pointing out that the club also became the League champions of this season with a lead of 11 points, and 24 of their 47 points for 30 matches had been gained away from home.

In this way did Aston Villa equal the dual achievement of Preston North End.

And this Villa team of Whitehouse; Spencer, Evans; Reynolds, Cowan (Jas.), Crabtree; Athersmith, Devey, Campbell (Jas.), Wheldon and Cowan (Jno.) must unquestionably be included among the finest elevens of all time.

In 1905 Aston Villa once again became the holders of the Cup, as they defeated Newcastle United, who made the first of their five appearances in seven consecutive seasons.

The Newcastle players could win the championship of the League and take all the four points possible in their matches with the Villa, but when they reached the valley at Sydenham they seemed to feel the shadow of defeat upon them.

This was not the Newcastle we had seen and applauded. Their players were overawed. Their efforts were laboured, and they appeared to be so self-conscious that they became helpless.

The centre-forward of the Villa, Hampton, was so fearless, so thrustful, so nimble and so troublesome to goalkeepers that no one could hold him in check.

Twice he scored, but even these goals did not represent the skill of the victors. Newcastle must have brought a hoodoo from Tyneside. And this dreadful spell must always have haunted them down in the Valley, for they never won a Final on that ground in three attempts.

The Newcastle club played sixteen men in these three games, Lawrence, Gardiner, McWilliam, Rutherford, Howie and Veitch taking part in all the games, Veitch appearing at inside-left, centre-forward and centre half-back.

There was always the nucleus of a winning team, but never could they escape the hoodoo.

On the other hand, Aston Villa's four appearances at the Crystal Palace all resulted in victories. They could not lose.

There was always that force of personality, of which I have written, in the elevens they placed on the field.

The Villa always had an electrical link in their Cup Finals. Howard Spencer, the big, silent back, was the link who handed on the vital force in 1895, 1897 and 1905. For eight years Hampton and Bache preserved that vital spark and communicated it to the team of 1913.

Aston Villa were always wonderful to me. Whatever match they were playing, the team tried to win by good football.

The directorate have been able to imbue their men with the idea that the reputation of the Villa is of the greatest importance.

If a footballer does not respond to this justifiable feeling of pride, with loyalty on the field and gentlemanly conduct off the field, he is not retained.

As we all know, Aston Villa have taken this Cup home six times. Once they mislaid or lost it. The F.A. had to purchase another Cup. That was first played for in 1896—the first Final that I was concerned with as secretary. This is by the way.

What people, as a rule, do not know is that in their six victorious Cup campaigns Aston Villa have scored 123 goals to 30. In 1886–87 their aggregate of goals was 40 to 10, in 1894–95 18 to 4, in 1896–97 17 to 6, in 1904–05 18 to 5, in 1912–13 20 to 2, and in 1919–20 10 to 3.

Looking at the matter in another way, these figures relate to 41 Cup-ties in which the Villa have averaged three goals and their opponents less than one.

Yet I cannot feel convinced that even the Aston Villa eleven of 1897 were quite as great in ball-play and craftsmanship as the old "Invincibles" of Preston.

This was the name that the public gave them, just as some perfervid admirers characterized the Sunderland combination of 1891–92–93 as "the team of all the talents."

The Northern towns have for half a century had excellent teams. This part of our country had such strength from 1906 to 1915 that the Cup never went to any club further south than Wolverhampton.

And Wolverhampton Wanderers, who routed Newcastle United in 1907–08, by the overpowering character of their first-class half-backs, were the second team from the Second Division to emerge as Cup conquerors.

This was at a time when transfer fees were limited to £350, when players' wages were £4 per week and when a bonus was illegal.

Is it any wonder that Mr. J.H. Addenbrooke, the secretary of the Wanderers, was very proud of a team that only cost in these fees just over £100?

About this period there was another Second Division team, Barnsley, that caused a great deal of commotion.

Here was a club virtually run by a big burly Yorkshireman, Mr. Arthur Fairclough, who had an extraordinary gift of picking up first-class players by the roadside, as it were.

We have heard much about modern managers, but there were wonderful men before the late Herbert Chapman conquered London and, shall I say, all England.

Mr. Fairclough had the practical mind and the discerning eye of a man who rears thoroughbreds and pedigree cattle, and he came from the same county as Chapman—Yorkshire.

Barnsley lived for years on the prize footballers they produced and sold to clubs with far more money than themselves.

Yet with all these transfers, and with never a thought of advancing into a higher grade, where they could not have maintained their membership, they got together, and held, an eleven that threatened to win the Cup for three years, and finally succeeded.

With the North at its strongest, they reached the Final in 1910. At the Palace they drew with Newcastle United, who won the replay at Everton, where the team from Tyneside felt at home, and in the second half abandoned elegance for stern but fair tackling.

Newcastle refused to be twice beaten by Second Division strength in three seasons.

In 1911 Barnsley fell before Burnley, who in turn were defeated by Bradford City, who, after drawing with Newcastle United, again at the Palace, were victors on the ground of Manchester United by a goal that was nodded by the back of the head of James Spiers, another good footballer slain in the Great War.

But in 1912 Barnsley were drawn against Bradford City, and they met thrice without either side scoring. At their fourth meeting Barnsley won by 3–2, and the Bradford City players had such admiration for their sturdy and skilful conquerors that they straightaway told them that they would like to see them win the Cup.

This they did, for after a goalless draw at the Palace Barnsley beat West Bromwich Albion at Bramell Lane ground, Sheffield, by a goal scored by Harry Tufnell, who played at inside-right and with fine control of a lively ball on a sun-baked ground, made a grand dribble that outwitted the Albion defenders, drew Hubert Pearson out of his goal and obliquely rolled the ball past him into the net.

Yorkshire gave a cheer that must have been a good imitation of the roar at Doncaster when the favourite wins the St. Leger.

Harold Pearson, Hubert's son, who also kept for the Albion, had better luck in 1931.

Tufnell partnered Wilfred Bartrop, the outside-right, who was quite the best forward in this match. He, too, was killed in the Great War, but he had joined Liverpool before "joining up for the duration," as we used to say in those dark days.

The calibre of this Barnsley team may be gauged from the fact that the full-back, Downs, the wing half-backs, Glendinning and Utley, and Bartrop and Lillycrop, of the forwards, were eventually transferred to First Division clubs.

Sheffield United, who took Utley, because they needed a captain, paid £2,000 for his services, this being the highest sum paid for a transfer up to that date—the middle of November, 1913.

I have always regarded Barnsley's victory as a miracle, and this opinion is confirmed by the failure of the club in Cup ties ever since 1912.

In 1931 they knocked out Sheffield Wednesday, but fell in the next or the fifth round.

Some most extraordinary results, or incidents unheard of, happen in most of the Cup tournaments, but Barnsley's display for three years is more amazing than a Derby winner at 100–1, because the effort was maintained for so long.

In post-war football there has been no parallel, although the three-fold victory of Bolton Wanderers, who began their hunt for the Cup somewhere about 1882–83, is remarkable, for they persevered through 40 years and failed in two Finals before their long trail was rewarded.

The only Southern League club that, as such, ever won the Cup was Tottenham Hotspur, and I have heard an official of this club say that they twice won the trophy in 1901.

The referee would not, of course, agree with that statement, but Hotspur did win handsomely in the replay against Sheffield United at Bolton.

In spite of the general view taken of the 1897 Final, it is doubtful to me if ever I watched such a display of what one may term diagram manœuvres or attacks in any match as that of Tottenham.

Sheffield United, then at their zenith, were made to look like an ordinary team being overplayed.

The torch which Tottenham lit burned away. After 20 years another torch was carried from Tottenham's broad highway to Chelsea's arena. And there other torches were lit from the flame of success.

In 1930 Arsenal again brought the Cup south, and West Ham, Cardiff and Portsmouth have striven to let their lights be seen by the crowds massed around Wembley's amphitheatre.

The engravers are waiting to imprint the names of new southern torch-bearers on the Cup.

CHAPTER XVIII

SOCCER'S GREATEST PLAYERS

WHEN I look back over my football life and try to recall the players who have left abiding impressions upon me I feel compelled to ask myself one question: "Has the game ever had another Alex James?" Frankly, I have never seen another.

Commenting upon the players of my time, that is over a period of more than 60 years, as an amateur, as a referee, and as an administrative official, I have either watched or been in touch with many of the most renowned footballers.

There are men still alive and still interested in the sport whose names are more or less familiar to this generation because of their footwork, their quick wits on the field, and their physical courage.

It is possible to choose from them an ideal England eleven, each man a master and the whole likely to blend.

This would, of course, be a purely imaginative combination based on the assumption that every one of these eleven was now at his physical best and playing at the height of his power as a footballer.

And yet, when I look at the names, the question arises: Is there an Alex James among them all? Not to my mind.

I am much concerned about the few really great footballers there are in these days. They are so battered about and played on that sympathy is aroused for them.

This is not a covert suggestion that football is played in a foul manner. Considering how valuable League points are to the club, and remembering the almost overpowering desire to win ties in the Association Cup tournament, the games are cleanly and fairly contested. There is plenty of vigour and robustness, but these are everyday experiences. There are few games in which force supersedes skill.

Nevertheless, an effective player, whose anticipation, ready power of observation and quick, decisive action, make him the driving wheel of the machine, becomes a marked man. How often has it been said that "we must stop" James, or David Jack, Buchan, "Billy" Walker, Clem Stephenson, Billy Gillespie?

In every good team there is a commanding personality, an extra good player, who is a leader. To the ordinary spectator the team may seem to excel because of its collective strength—but the players know the man whose influence is felt, whose tactics and shrewd touches mean so much to the eleven. He is always a marked man.

But Alex James never suppresses himself. He may conceal his intention, he may lead a man away on the wrong trail, he may hold the ball and invite a tackle, he may fool an opponent who becomes ruffled, and he may do the most unexpected thing in a flash, but he does not seem to care what may happen to himself.

Do not be deluded by any praise bestowed upon the most celebrated men of former days, or by the prejudiced criticism of this day.

Alex James is the greatest of all the outstanding players of his period, and, in my judgment, he would have been just as masterful, whimsical, and self-possessed in any period when football has been an organized, collective and disciplined game.

I live more in the present than in the past. I am confident I have never seen another James, and it would be almost foolish to be sanguine of any club ever discovering his like.

It is customary for club managers and writers for newspapers to speak of A, B, or C as "another James"; as the material likely to develop into "another James."

Without being either cynical or sceptical, I shall only believe there is "another James" when he presents himself in action.

Apart from his trickery, juggling and ball control in little space, his ability to scheme, open up the game and set the forwards galloping, there is the mental equipment of the man.

He is a Scotsman.

James is a man of extraordinary self-possession. He never loses himself—and rarely the ball. You may take the ball from him—if you can—but he never gives it.

This equanimity of mind is a tremendous asset. Excitement does not appear to be part of his make-up. However he may be played on, rolled on the ground, battered and bruised, hampered and hustled, he never betrays the least trace of resentment. If he has such a feeling it never can be inferred from his actions. However he may be nudged or buffeted, he picks himself up and goes on with the business he has to do.

The reader may say that a little fellow of 5 ft. 6 in., and under 11 stone, could not afford to be hasty in temper and resentful. That may be or may not be, but he is keen on what he believes to be his rights, and he can be stubborn. Yet on the field he is a model, and if there were 22 like him in a match the referee could be dispensed with.

His control of himself is as great a gift to him as his control of the ball. Nature's bounty and his own industry have made him the footballer he is. Such a combination is rare, and that is why I despair of ever again looking upon his like.

He makes opportunities by gathering stray balls. Roberts, the centre half-back of Arsenal, once said to an interviewer (at least, I read it) that, when he got the ball, his desire was to pass it to James and "leave the rest to him."

What confidence such a forward can give to a side! No wonder that he is so helpful as captain.

There is, however, another side to this man that I cannot overlook. By the deceptive daring of his manœuvres he makes spectators laugh. To make fifty or sixty thousand people laugh when the tension is great and the spirit of partisanship is abroad is a great gift—nay, almost a blessing.

As a rule our spectacular team games are far too serious. The footballer who becomes an entertainer without sacrificing efficiency provides an antidote to prejudice and passion.

Many enthusiasts must remember Alan Morton of Glasgow Rangers. Turn back in memory to the last day of March, 1928, and recall the forward line of Scotland against England at Wembley. With Jackson (Huddersfield), Dunn (Edinburgh Hibernians), Gallacher (Newcastle United), James (Preston North End) and Morton (Rangers), Scotland had a set of forwards that gained a tremendous victory. Those men scored five goals. There were good half-backs, but the ball-control and shooting of these five will always be remembered. James, who scored twice in that match, revealed himself as a marksman. He is still a good shot. Does not the reader remember the first goal of the Final tie of 1930, when James made a shot beyond the power of man to stop?

Of course, James did not take all the glory to himself. He ran to Clifford Bastin and shook his hand. Probably Bastin has never had a handshake so eloquent in appreciation of team-work.

James had just as high a sense of comradeship when the wee Morton was his partner. How well many of these little chaps can play! If Scotland ever had a better pair on the left wing than James and Morton, I never saw them.

Morton played in as many matches against England as Bobby Walker, of the Heart of Midlothian. Although only 5 ft. 3½ in. and at least half a stone lighter than James, this bonny raider would go right up to any back.

If James be the most brilliant and original professional of modern times, surely Morton once occupied a similar position among amateurs, although he eventually changed his status.

In the sense that he was a paid player for Glasgow Rangers, Morton was a professional; but he adhered to the style that he acquired with Queen's Park and relied entirely upon the talent tucked away in his ten toes.

Although born in a suburb of Glasgow, Morton was brought up on a farm at Shotts, one of a family of five boys and three girls, who all played football together on the farm fields.

Football was in the blood, and was developed at the academy of Airdrie and with "the Queen's" or "the Spiders," as they were formerly called.

I suppose this nickname was an allusion to what the spider is reported to have said to the fly, for clubs who walked into the old Hampden Park ground had the same experience as the proverbial fly.

I said "ten toes" because Alan Morton had the use of both feet. He could play at outside-right, but his fame lives because he was an outside-left who did so much with his right foot. In this he resembled Spikesley.

Most dexterous as a dribbler, he was helped by the elusiveness of his small body, which he could swerve like a schoolmaster's cane.

To tackle him was difficult. His opponent went for the tackle but only made the air wave. Morton's brain was quick to see a situation, and his feet swiftly adept in working it out.

Shooting or delivering centres with either foot, he was a dandy player, as the Scots say. He studied the game and was never a haphazard raider who trusted to providence when he released the ball.

It was said that Alec McNair, of the Celtic, could hold him, but he was about as studious as Morton. I cannot recall an English back who mastered this little, quiet, modest man.

Our Selection Committee were always trying to work out a scheme for checking Morton. Once they introduced a plan of playing Magee, "Maggie" they called him at West Bromwich, at left half-back, with Wadsworth, of Huddersfield, behind him, but my recollection is that neither of them could capture Morton, who had his club mate, Tom Cairns, of the Rangers, for partner. England never scored, and Scotland won by two goals. The Scots were too clever. England has never had anyone who could counter Morton's moves, that were so difficult to foresee.

Some of these Scotsmen, so clever with the ball, linger in the memory. Morton has reminded me of Robert Templeton, who was universally known as "Bobby." He, too, was a man who had perfect use of either foot. There never was such a classical example of the value of a player with two trained feet as Templeton.

Thirty years ago he was chosen to play as outside-left for

Scotland against England at Glasgow. He was then a Newcastle player, and his fellow countryman, Thomas Niblo, was placed at outside-right. This was a curious choice, because Niblo was a left-footed player.

As outside-right, Niblo was anything but a success. At the interval the Scottish selectors placed Templeton at outside-right and Niblo at outside-left. They reversed positions. Niblo, who was clever and speedy, was better in his accustomed position, but not so telling as he could be.

Templeton was not the dazzling raider we knew him to be in either position, for he was confronted, first by Crompton and next by Herbert Burgess, and he was unable to do as he wished.

Under these circumstances England won, for Bloomer, then drawing towards the close of his international career, scored an excellent goal.

Nevertheless, Templeton stands out as a man able to acquit himself with credit on either wing in the internationial match of the season in Great Britain.

Well built, for he stood 5 ft. 9 in. and weighed a little over 11 stones, Templeton arrested attention, as he was rather good looking. In this day we should say that his hair had a permanent wave, but 30 years ago this phrase had not become a vogue.

A striking personality, he was a man of many clubs, and no one, either before or since his day, had such a pair of twinkling feet when dribbling a ball, and that at a thrilling pace.

He was described as a gazelle, as a wizard and a juggler. He could do anything he liked with a ball, and tossing it from one foot to the other, he was regarded as the most artistic and sparkling dribbler that even Scotsmen had ever seen.

No doubt he had his moods, but on his day no one could approach him, and his fanciful exposition of ball play was then the despair of his foes. Those who were jealous of his ability said he was a sand-dancer, but he was an artistic dodger and could centre with any man.

Elusive and showy, he was a rare player, whose sudden death in November, 1919, awoke a flood of recollections. He is still remembered both in England and Scotland, especially in his native Ayrshire, a county that has produced so many players who have cast a spell over the crowd upon many a winter's day.

I have taken three Scottish forwards as examples of the characteristic style of the footballer of that country. There are many others who could be cited as typical ball players, but I wish to pay a tribute to other parts of the British Isles.

In recent years, that is, since 1919-20, Wales has played a prominent part in the game, for the Principality has in five seasons placed on the field the champion international eleven, whereas it had only once won in pre-war contests, in 1906-07. There is no stronger proof of the development of our game on scientific lines.

One player represented Wales more than any other man. Of course I refer to William Meredith, with the accent on the second syllable. In his native land he was called Me-red-ith.

Born a short distance inside the Border, he was inclined to lament that he was not an Englishman. He played for his country from 1895 until 1920, and took part in more international games of the standard series than any other man.

For many years he used to say that he would like to live long enough to be, for once, on the winning side against England.

The day he longed for came after the Great War, for he played in the "Victory" international match at Cardiff in October, 1919, when Wales defeated England by 2–1, and he scored the first goal.

This, however, was considered an "unofficial" match, but in the official match at Highbury the following year, when Wales prevailed by the same score, he was in his accustomed position.

On both occasions he was very pleased, but at Cardiff, England in the second half had only ten men, and at Highbury Wales obtained their first goal from the penalty-kick spot for "hands" against Pennington—a decision that was not universally approved at the time.

Still, Meredith's long trail was ended, for this was the first win of Wales since February, 1881, when the late Mr. L. Llewelyn Kenrick, the first Secretary of the Football Association of Wales, in an emergency played in his ordinary boots and trousers, and played well. At least, that is the story handed down to us by some of the veterans of ancient days.

Although born at Chirk, the nursery of Welsh football, and taught football by the local schoolmaster, Mr. T.E. Thomas, Meredith never spoke Welsh, and he was "hot and bothered" when compatriots began to shower congratulations and compliments upon him in their native Celtic tongue. He seemed more annoyed than pleased, but his mixed feelings can easily be understood.

More of a footballer than a linguist, he was one of the greatest outside-rights who ever played. There can be argument without end when the champions of W.I. Bassett, "Jocky" Simpson and Meredith meet.

A man who always kept himself in perfect condition by an abstemious life, his sole method of training was ball practice. Being spare of habit and lean in limb, two days a week sufficed to keep him fit for the game during 25 years.

An expert dribbler, blessed with sufficient speed, he hugged the touch line, and very often took the ball up to the corner flag before making his centre. His defence of going so far was that all his fellow forwards were on-side when they were behind the ball. This was good logic, even if it be not a fashionable plan in these days.

Not only was he a great dribbler, but he was crafty and cunning in hoodwinking opponents. No man was ever more wary of the outstretched leg for a trip. He hopped over the trap as if it was a twig.

Of the back-heel pass he was a ready exponent, and he remains the only man I have ever seen chewing a quill toothpick while playing in the hardest of matches. Indeed, his toothpick was just as characteristic of him as his bandy legs.

In his day he was a splendid raider, and one of the Manchester City directors, Mr. Joshua Parlby, always declared that he should have been a centre-forward. Possibly goalkeepers were thankful that he was not, for he obtained over 200 goals from outside-right.

A good story relates to the Wales v. England match on Wrexham racecourse, in 1908. It was disastrous to Wales, for that was the occasion when L.R. Roose was injured, and in the second half Dai Davies was allowed to keep goal.

Evelyn Lintott, the talented schoolmaster, who was so fine a left half-back, played in all the big matches of 1907-08, and on this occasion he was ordered never to leave Meredith. He clung to him like an affectionate brother.

At last the patience of Meredith gave out and he turned on Lintott with these words: "Go away, you confounded schoolboy. Go away! Do you hear? You have got seven cursed goals, how many more do you want?"

Lintott was silent, but he continued to haunt his jaded adversary. Wales have had lots of fine players, but their football prince remains Meredith the magnificent.

CHAPTER XIX

WIZARDS OF WALES AND IRELAND

GALLANT Wales has had many valiant sons, but William Meredith stands pre-eminent because of his long service and high skill. Without being a braggart, Meredith was jealous of the new men who stepped over the touch line.

When "Jocky" Simpson linked up with the Blackburn Rovers, he was, quite justifiably, praised to the skies. Some critics declared that he was the superior of Bassett and Meredith.

One day a daring enquirer ventured to ask the Welsh chieftain what he thought of Simpson. Meredith turned his toothpick round and about before he replied: "Let's see how long he keeps it up. Tell me, what will he be like when he has had my years of service?"

There was no attempt to decry Simpson, but a suggestion that stamina and endurance were attributes that should be considered when rank was being determined.

These two men were of different types, physically and temperamentally, for Simpson was small and plump, Meredith taller and lean; Simpson had a sonsie, contented face, Meredith a countenance that made a man think that life had not been too happy for him.

As footballers there were differences, for Simpson was more of the Scottish type in control and more given to cutting past the right hand of the back and using his left foot for shooting.

Meredith could no doubt have done the same, but his general preference was to pull the ball back from the corner flag.

Simpson anticipated the modern method of converging

goalwards and being ever ready for a cross-kick from the left wing. It was this ball, taken with his left instep, that gave Simpson so many goals.

If I were taking an all-British eleven for a long tour in a distant part of the Empire and Meredith were young and fit, I should prefer him to "Jocky" Simpson, as he would be the more likely to wear well. For "an occasion," as we say, I would like to have Simpson on my side.

There have been other Welshmen of great fame— such as L.R. Roose, the bacteriologist, who was such a sensation as a goalkeeper. A clever man, he had what is sometimes described as the eccentricity of genius. His daring was seen in the goal, where he was often taking risks and emerging triumphant. Going to the war, he never returned. Presumably he took a risk once too often.

Wales have had a succession of very fine men at centre half-back. The methods of Cæsar Augustus Llewellyn Jenkyns, the stimulating presence and voice of Colonel M. Morgan-Owen, the Corinthian, the high spirit and never-say-die endurance of Fred Keenor, and the dominating style and shrewd tactics of T.P. Griffiths as pivots of the Welsh teams will never be forgotten.

Caesar Jenkyns, who belonged to the era when players wore moustaches, was a strong fellow, who used to throw his weight about in days when the charge was more common than now. He commanded, shall I say, respect, the same as did Moses Russell. Jenkyns was considered the mainstay of Small Heath for seven or eight years, and played for his country whenever he was available.

Morgan-Owen, who got his colours both at Shrewsbury School and when he went up to Oriel College, Oxford, enjoyed every minute of his football and was a cheery leader on international days.

"Come on, boys, play up!" was his slogan.

How gallantly he played in the England and Wales match at Fuiham in 1907, when some of his fellow patriots thought that they had really won! The match was drawn, but Meredith considered that Wales got a legitimate goal that the referee did not allow.

Of the same high spirit and rallying power as Morgan-Owen

was Fred Keenor, an admirable captain, and so clever with the ball and so zealous for his country that Wales had to play him when he was really beyond his best. Keenor, too, enjoyed his games.

How fortunate were Wales that, when Keenor had to quit the field he adorned, his place could be taken by T.P. Griffiths, who is, I should say, probably the best footballer that the country has ever had in the position.

There is, however, one other Welsh player that I cannot pass by without a tribute.

It is the fashion to pretend that Wales has only had one really great player—William Meredith—but this is nonsense, probably due to the fleeting nature of popularity. For a variety of reasons, it seems to me that a fine cricketer holds his place in our memories much longer than an equally fine footballer. The man I am thinking of is Grenville Morris, who retired from the game when still active in the spring of 1913. He had played for Nottingham Forest about fifteen seasons. In that period he scored over 200 goals from inside-left and probably "made" as many more for his comrades.

He was the captain of Wales in 1906-07, when that country first won the British championship of Association football.

Spouncer, who played for England against Wales in 1900, was lucky to have such an inside partner as Morris in his club games.

Playing as centre-forward for Wales, when eighteen years old, it is highly probable that he would have rivalled Meredith in the number of his appearances in international games had he been as eager for caps. He became a professional but in spirit was always an amateur, and he was unquestionably a footballer who played a clean and chivalrous game. As an inside-left he had for years no superior.

He applied to be reinstated when his club, Nottingham Forest, would have continued his engagement. His application was not granted. A first-class lawn tennis player, the Notts Lawn Tennis Association supported his request.

The committee, however, could not see their way to reinstate him, as he had been a paid player for about sixteen years. That was the deciding factor, for in all else he was an artist with a consummate touch and a spotless record.

His recreations were lawn tennis and chess. The one trained his body in the close season and the table game appealed to his mental faculties.

I have often thought that lawn tennis gives a great amount of hard exercise, and would be a helpful variation to the ordinary routine of training. There have been men who, with intimate knowledge of both games, have declared that a singles match, the best of five sets, was often as much a test of fitness and stamina as any football match. Possibly that is why the trainer of a club prefers golf for a change.

When I set myself to recall some of the Irish players who have lent lustre to our game, the first man who comes to mind is William Gillespie.

Can the reader imagine what a trial Irish players passed through for a period of over thirty years when they met England? Never had they the encouragement of a victory from 1882 to 1912. They must have thought that the fates were against them.

Twice had our friendly foes across the water experienced the depression of counting thirteen goals by Englishmen. Even when those days were left behind the Irish teams often played well at Belfast, but could never do better than draw.

Yet they were always optimistic and rare triers. Over and over again they began a match with such dash that they seemed as if they intended to win in half an hour. Generally they could not maintain the pace they set, and England kept up her sequence of successes.

Thirty years and ne'er a win for Ireland! Some of their greybeards must have moaned as they looked at the printed record and said, "How long, how long? My heart bleeds for her. We have beaten Wales and even Scotland. But England never. How long?"

There came a day in the middle of February, 1913, when Ireland and England met once again at the foot of Cave Hill and the Saxon invaders were beaten. The ground is known as Windsor Park, but the English eleven could not delude themselves into fancying they were in their own country.

When Charles Buchan, England's inside-right, headed a goal from a corner-kick, the point almost passed unnoticed. When William Gillespie rendered the scores equal there was a demonstration like a clap of thunder, but this was a faint sound compared with the fortissimo of the salvo that greeted another goal, early in the second half, by the same Gillespie.

Pistols were fired, trumpets were blown, rattles were sounded, jigs were danced, and, in short, such pandemonium reigned that even the tall and stolid men of the Royal Irish Constabulary looked on the crowd with anxious eyes.

England tried desperately to save their prestige. All in vain, for the forwards fiddled away their chances and when the referee signalled "time" a wild wave of Irishmen surged across the field to the small pavilion that contained what some players have called the "stripping rooms."

The crowd was bursting with joy and good humour, even if there were some desperate struggles to take the wooden shelter by storm.

When the English eleven regained their quarters some of the forwards were not happy; one was bitter and another was almost in tears. And yet some people say that English footballers are so phlegmatic that they cannot evince patriotic feeling.

Still, I never knew a team that suffered defeat gladly, and if footballers neither cherish our national prestige nor their own prestige, how can anyone explain why many English professionals have preferred a gold medal as their reward, rather than the fee they were entitled to?

As I consider William Gillespie, the hero of Irish international football in modern times, and for years the brain and cold calculator of Sheffield United, it becomes necessary to emphasize these views, for football folks, as a rule, are not hoarders of recollections apart from their club or one favourite player.

The victory of Ireland in 1913 was due to Gillespie, who was playing in his first international match, and was all the more noteworthy because Macaulay, of Huddersfield, a fine forward, was injured and unable to play during the last hour. Gillespie always proved himself to be at his best when the best was needed and defeat threatened. Always a tactician, he thought out a match. Ten years after Ireland's historic victory the Hibernian host again won on the same ground, when Gillespie was the captain and had only another forward of established reputation in Irvine, of Everton, by his side.

The disappointments of the Irish F.A. selectors were so many that Brown, of Tranmere Rovers, and Croft, of Queen's Island, had to be the right-wing, and Toner, of Arsenal, the outside-left. Even Irishmen said, "Who's Brown?" and "Where the divvil is Tranmere? Is it on the map?"

Yet Gillespie planned his campaign like the general he always was, and got a goal—he was always scoring against England. And then Croft, one of the unknown, shot the winning goal. He was so cool and confident that Gillespie, his captain, simply stood still and watched him.

Gillespie, the least excitable of Irishmen, according to all accounts threw restraint to the winds, for, as he afterwards said, he felt certain that England were about to be beaten for the second time.

Gillespie showed just the same generalship when Sheffield United won the Association Cup at Wembley in 1925.

He was a first-class forward in any position, but probably his best place was at inside-left. Very often he hung behind the forward line, like Alex James, and was a great collector of stray balls.

There was, however, a marked difference between Gillespie and James, for the Irishman was a schemer with one touch and not a dribbler, as a rule. He could dribble, but his contention was that there was always a possibility of losing the ball when dribbling.

He preferred the one touch that he learned from that superb footballer Ernest Needham, who, as an adviser, first instilled into him the wisdom of letting the ball travel alone instead of piloting it.

This young man from Londonderry, who went from Leeds City to Sheffield United, had a quiet, thoughtful face, surmounted by jet black hair.

After breaking a leg in the first match of 1914-15, he enlisted "for the duration." After five years' absence, he returned to Sheffield United with furrows in his face and nearly bald. Yet, with all his limbs intact, he was fitter than ever and even a more telling schemer. What testimony Frederick Tunstall could pay him!

And the late John Nicholson, the secretary of Sheffield United, once wrote of Gillespie in a private letter:

"He has taken his ups and downs in a playing sense quite calmly and has done his best, whichever team he has been selected for, and he has had experience of both."

The evenness of his temperament, whether in war or peace, was the secret of his long career. That is why he returned a better player than ever.

There have been many fine Irish footballers from the days of W.K. Gibson, the Cliftonville amateur, to the farewell of Elisha Scott, their justly renowned goalkeeper, but I take Gillespie as the sovereign example.

Many lovers of Association football are passionately fond of selecting teams for their country from present-day players. Others like to choose an eleven for All Britain—first from the present and then from the past. Then they endeavour to make a blend of the past and present and argue about the relative merits of their favourites. The discussion never brings agreement.

Sometimes I think of the match at Sheffield in 1920, when England won by 5–4. That was a fine game in the mud. One man out of the rival teams has appeared in first-class football this season. I refer to Robert Kelly, a consistently good and neat player.

Then one jumps back to England's "old crocks," who won so handsomely at Glasgow in 1892, and sees again some of the England and Scotland matches at Kennington Oval.

From this medley of matches I pick a team, on the supposition that all the men are with us and fit to play. My speculations result in this eleven as embodying England's best, not merely of individual excellence, but of collective capacity:—

Sutcliffe (Bolton Wanderers), goal; Crompton (Blackburn Rovers), Pennington (West Bromwich Albion), backs; Crabtree

(Aston Villa), N.C. Bailey (Old Westminsters), Needham (Sheffield United), half-backs; Bassett (West Bromwich Albion), Bloomer (Derby County), V.J. Woodward (Tottenham Hotspurs), W.N. Cobbold (Old Carthusians) and E.C. Bambridge (Swifts), forwards. The team is intended to read from the right to left sides of the field.

I realize that these great players do not include a post-war celebrity apart from Pennington, although Crompton did make an occasional appearance. They are the backs I prefer, because they never let England down.

Sutcliffe, of course, had the benefit of a Rugby football training, was a superb fielder, and although fully 5 ft. 10½ in., he would, in desperate situations, pick the ball off a forward's boot and with a strong punt or a drop-kick place it among his own forwards. He seemed to know where the shot would come from. A fearless 'keeper, he was almost without reproach.

As a Rugbeian he once kicked a goal from his own "25" yards line!

Possibly James Crabtree was the finest all-round player of his day, for he took all the five positions among the backs in international games. He did not know his own resources until Mr. F.W. Rinder, of Aston Villa, insisted upon experiments.

Like Sutcliffe, Norman C. Bailey played both codes of football, and as he was about 5 ft. 9 in. and 12 stones in weight he was built for tackling. As a centre half-back he showed judgment and agility and was universally considered a magnificent footballer. No wonder that he played for ten consecutive years against Scotland, who were exceedingly strong.

It was a toss-up whether Crabtree or Needham was the better, player. Both were natural footballers of the highest class.

Of Bassett, Bloomer and Woodward I have previously written. They have not had superiors as a group in these positions.

"Nuts" Cobbold and "Charlie" Bambridge belong to the middle of the Victorian 'eighties, and were contemporaries of Norman Bailey. Cobbold learned to dribble in the new Charterhouse School, where he went in 1877, and got his colours as well as his Blue at Cambridge, where he was distinguished as a captain.

At school he played on a hard ground, bare of grass as a rule, and with twenty or thirty boys on each side. Dribbling the ball closely under such conditions was the training that made him the greatest of dribblers, for he never passed until compelled. He combined many good qualities, not the least being that of marksmanship and the ability to take care of himself.

Cobbold and Bambridge formed the best left wing of their era. They showed what men with quick thinking and quick and trained feet could do. They were both fast and had the same style.

I am convinced that Bambridge would have held his own in any era; and do not forget that he played eighteen times for England and figured in many a hard match against Preston North End.

In a comparatively recent interview I remember that Bambridge said that the Preston eleven were excellent in all positions, very clever and unique in "dovetailing." The Corinthians often played them.

But the most robust match and the cleverest opponents never troubled Bambridge. When he played his first match against Wales he was 8 st. 5 lb., and he was never more than 10 st. 5 lb. But he was never known to funk.

He was one of five brothers, all good footballers (three of international rank) and true sportsmen. As one of the younger members of the family, he had excellent examples to follow.

I have never met a more cheery soul than "Charlie" Bambridge, who has always maintained that football should be just a jolly good game played for bodily recreation and mental refreshment.

Nevertheless, my England eleven, if it could be assembled (eight are still on this planet), would, I am sure, cause a profound impression by their play, even in these days of goal-packing and safety first.

CHAPTER XX

FOOTBALL OVER EUROPE

THE average man who takes an interest in football has only the faintest idea how the game began to be played on the other side of the English Channel. The "noxious weed," as some of our Rugby friends have called the Association game, was sown and transplanted in various lands and in several ways.

Boys who have been educated in England have returned to their homes on the Continent with some rudimentary knowledge of the winter revel, and a football under their arm.

One of the Rothschilds sent a gardener to England to study the culture of trees and flowers, and he went back with the knowledge he required and another football under his arm.

Do they not say that the Britons working at the Rio Tinto mines in Southern Spain, and others in a somewhat similar business at Bilbao, set the ball rolling in the peninsula? Boys and men in many countries have scattered the seed and this has mostly fallen on fruitful ground. For many reasons football makes a universal appeal.

The Danes and the Dutch certainly adopted what we call "our game" in 1889. Belgium and Switzerland followed their example about 1895, and Italy began in 1898, when foreigners played in the North—that is, in Piedmont and Lombardy. These "foreigners" were mostly English and Swiss.

An Oxford University team visited Central Europe, Bohemia and Austria about 1875. The game gradually grew in various parts, and English club teams, amateur in particular, made many holiday excursions on the Continent, the Middlesex Wanderers being frequent visitors.

The Football Association and the Corinthians sent teams to these countries, but only Denmark, Holland, Belgium, Switzerland and Italy had taken up the pastime before this century. The great development has been since 1900, and more particularly after peace was restored to Europe in 1919.

Mr. Thomas Atkins, in France, Flanders, and Salonika, dribbling a football into battle, or behind the line in rest camps, was the one man who gave the final great and broad impetus to the game.

The trend of the game on the Continent has been on international lines, and by this I mean to suggest that the matches between different countries are held to be far more important than club championships. National pride and prestige are great motive forces.

Yet these representative contests are very modern institutions. Austria and Hungary began to play such matches in 1902, Belgium and France in 1904, Holland and Switzerland in 1905, Denmark, Germany, Norway and Sweden in 1908, Italy in 1910, Czechoslovakia and Spain in 1920, and Turkey in 1923.

So strong a grip has the international match got that Hungary and Sweden have each played over 170 matches against various adversaries, Austria over 150, Belgium over 140, France and Holland over 120, Switzerland over 114, and Italy nearly 110. These facts and figures show how popular the game has become abroad. And it is intensely international in tone.

Nor must I overlook the fact that two of the Continental associations have the right to use the prefix "royal," for the title was granted by King Albert to the Belgian body in February, 1920, and by Queen Wilhelmina to the Dutch F.A. in November, 1929.

The governing associations in Great Britain have not yet risen to this dignity, perhaps because the service which such a national game renders to the United Kingdom is not fully recognized. Nearly every one of these associations in Europe has been "recognized by the Government."

These countries across the English Channel all desire to play

England—the pioneers of the modern phase of the game. We are not fellow-members of the Fédération Internationale de Football Association, which consists of the controlling authority from each country, all other organizations being excluded.

The Football Association became a member of the Federation in 1906, on the understanding, as recorded in an official minute, that "the Football Association should use their influence to regulate football on the Continent as a pure sport and to give all Continental associations the full benefit of their many years' experience."

The football of the European mainland then was in such a state that England could send a team to most countries and stop counting after scoring ten goals.

The F.A., years ago, withdrew from the Federation—not merely because the two bodies could not agree upon the definition of an amateur, but because there was an undercurrent of feeling that the Federation should exercise world-control of all football.

The relations of Great Britain and the Federation are quite amicable, but England, Scotland, Ireland and Wales prefer their own self-government and insist upon the laws of the game being made, and revised if necessary, by an International Board of the four countries and two representatives of the Federation.

Any resolution of this Board could not become operative unless agreed to by four-fifths of those present. This means that the Federation could throw the deciding weight into the scale if Great Britain were not unanimous.

The idea is to keep the privilege of making the laws of the game in the hands of those countries which have been playing since 1863, when the various rules of the Association game were drafted into one code of paramount principles. We want to govern ourselves both on and off the field.

So far, Europe and Great Britain have conformed to one code—although there are interpretations and customs on the Continent that do not obtain in these islands.

The countries of the Continent have so greatly advanced in the playing of the game, having for many years been taught by professionals from Britain, that we have said "Good-bye" to all the nonsense about the stopping of counting after British teams have scored ten goals.

The position has changed, for of late years the standard of Continental football has become very high. This should be recognized by British clubs who wish to play matches against Continental clubs and to make a tour.

The day is past when these trips can be taken as a holiday after a long and arduous season of League matches and Cup ties. Again and again the plea has been advanced that when English or Scottish teams visit these countries the players are tired and stale, and that they do not take these matches too seriously.

Their opponents are lit and eager to win, and the spectators want to see a genuine and hard-fought game, with both sides striving desperately for victory. There have been many complaints that the visiting teams do not respond to these desires.

Then why go? Why take a club eleven that is fatigued and virtually unfit to fulfil a contract? Such displays as they give and the defeats they sustain do discredit to this or any other country.

Every club sending a team abroad has to apply for the consent of the Football Association at least fourteen days before the intended matches or tour, and the F.A. inform the foreign associations when consent has been given. The F.A., however, do not take any responsibility for the calibre or condition of the team.

There is no wish, so far as I know, to stop these club tours, or intervene in any way, but it does seem to me that the directors of a club should not undertake such a programme unless they have fit players and a reasonable hope of giving their opponents a good game and the spectators sport worth watching.

Turning to international contests between England and the Continental countries, there are other points of view. We take an English eleven when the season has been concluded. We go when the players are not completely out of condition, but when they are deprived of their full vigour and freshness.

Naturally men vary, but the F.A. take the best available team in the judgment of the International Selection Committee.

It has been the practice of the F.A. to take abroad in May, when possible, the team that has played against Scotland. While no definite promise has been made, it is understood that if the players win against Scotland they may be chosen for the Continental tour which follows.

The men are always keen to be included, and they have had the advantage of having played together and developed a sense of comradeship.

In 1933 it was not possible to take to Rome, for the match with Italy, the eleven that met Scotland at Glasgow, but England had a fine side and I never saw a better game. Italy had a great team of athletes, who had trained and practised together, whereas England's eleven had had no such opportunity, and yet they drew.

The customs of England and Italy differ. Most Continental countries prepare and train their men for international events. If the sole selector for Italy wishes, he can assemble his team, take the men away from their clubs to some quiet, exhilarating retreat, and keep them under his eyes until the match is decided.

The club and the player must obey the order if the man is fit. For disobedience a fine can be inflicted upon both club and player.

What is true of Italy is true of other countries. There is no trifling where the honour of Italy, or Austria, or Hungary, let us say, is concerned.

The viewpoint is entirely different. Abroad, international sport has a political aspect. Football in England is not carried on for the purposes of playing a foreign country and gaining a victory. Football in dear old England is merely a sporting entertainment.

It is true that our clubs compete for what we may call prizes. Still, spectacular football, so far as the people are concerned, aye, and so far as the Government is concerned, is just an entertainment. The clubs pay the Entertainment Tax just as much as a theatre.

England regards an international match as a game, but Continental countries look upon one of these matches as a test of strength, spirit and skill. Victory increases national prestige and defeat is a sign of decadence. To them success is vital.

When the match was played at Rome, it was stated that Signor Mussolini had promised the Italian players a considerable sum for a draw and double the amount for a win. He was, however, so pleased with the drawn game that he presented each member of the team with the money he had offered for a win. This was said to be equal to £16 each in English currency.

In Great Britain there is an agreement between the associations of the United Kingdom to pay a fixed fee of six guineas for an international match. Although the players receive their six guineas per match when abroad, they have been given a gratuity after the tour is over.

The International Selection Committee at a meeting voted the men who played at Rome, and at Berne against Switzerland, a sum of twelve guineas each—the extra money being a gratuity for good play and good conduct.

This was not a bonus offered in advance and contingent upon results, for the F.A. have never acted on that principle. England drew at Rome and won at Berne, but the results did not prompt the gratuity, which was an expression of appreciation. Even after the matches England lost at Budapest and Prague last May, the Association gave a gratuity of ten shillings a day for the twelve days abroad.

Readers will have noticed that Italy relies upon one man for the constitution of her teams. He is Signor Vittorio Pozzo, who has been an amateur player and an ardent enthusiast since his youth. He has lived in England, knows English methods, and is indeed well acquainted with the football of the world.

Almost as much may be said for Hugo Meisl, of Vienna, the secretary, and as he is described, the assistant-captain to the Austrian Football Union. These men have been the power behind Italian and Austrian football.

They have been the one selector of their national teams and have shepherded them. Can any one say that either has failed? In recent seasons Austria and Italy have been regarded as the champions of Europe. The play of their representative teams has been universally admired.

I have been asked the question: Why not a sole selector for England? One naturally replies: Find the man. As this may not be considered a satisfactory answer, and as I do not wish to sit on the fence, I may say that I would not put such a responsibility on the shoulders of one man—but of three men.

Have we a Pozzo or a Meisl in this country? Has any other country a Pozzo or a Meisl? Has the one-selector system had a general trial on the Continent? I understand that it has not.

The International Selection Committee of the Football Association consists of eleven men, apart from the chairman and vice-chairman of the Council, who are members of all Standing Committees. It is generally agreed that large committees are not smooth-working machines.

Their choice of men is popularly supposed to be unanimous. Some followers of football may wonder whether that is fact or fable. No matter, the only point worth emphasizing is that each team is selected as the best available.

For my part, however, I feel that a committee of three might take into consultation and confidence two men of reputation amongst the club managers, two men who have the best knowledge of players in every respect.

A heavy responsibility rests upon the officers of the Football Association, for they constitute all the committees. It must be difficult to appoint the most experienced and suitable officers for each special duty, and particularly for the construction of national teams.

I repeat, would it not be well to consult representative managers from the North and the South? We have had the example of England's selectors at cricket seeking the opinions of Hobbs and Rhodes. Surely if that could be done in cricket, with all its conservatism, such a plan should not be impossible in football?

To do so would not be a reflection upon the committee. It would not be derogatory to their dignity, because after all, they are, like other people, merely taking advice.

There has never been, so far as I know, a team that has been welcomed with unanimous approval before a match. If the men win, then they are praised and sometimes talked about for many years after the event. The public have a way of waiting for the result and then propounding their wise remarks and theories.

They little know, in fact they never know, the player who gets a cap by an odd vote, or those who have not found sufficient favour.

And, in my judgment, the larger the committee the greater the confusion of thought. Italy and Austria have been fortunate to find a Pozzo and a Meisl and to feel sure that the autocratic power given to them will not be misapplied.

As England has no such team-builder, I believe in a small committee with power to call in experts. Even doctors have been known to meet specialists in consultation.

Since this century came in, England has only won nine games against Scotland in 30 matches. That is not satisfactory, especially when we know that our best players are quite as good as the Scots.

The late Mr. "Johnny" McDowall used to say, in a whisper, that if "we" (the Scottish Association, for whom he was secretary) chose the best, "we" should always win. The perfect example of the optimist. If England always won, there would not be any interest in the match.

Nevertheless, we ought to have a more inspiriting record than that I have mentioned.

I find that England has played 29 matches against eleven of the most powerful footballing countries in Europe since 1921— that is, all post-war football. Her chosen have won 21 of these matches, lost four and drawn four.

Only five of these games have been played in England, where defeat has never been sustained. The only country to get more than a goal against England when playing at home has been Austria, who played so well in the second half of the match at Chelsea in 1932.

In these 29 matches England has obtained 107 goals and lost 43, the figures at home in the Old Country being 26–6. Surely this is a record to be proud of. It makes me wonder why English teams do not play so well as they can against Scotland.

The only defeats of England in these Continental tours have been at Madrid in 1929, Paris in 1931, and Budapest and Prague in 1934. The mystery match was that at Paris—but to err is human.

Probably the finest Continental eleven that England ever met was that of Italy at Rome.

So far as the experience of England's teams goes, there has never been any cause for complaint about either the grounds or the crowds on the Continent. At Stockholm, Berlin and Rome there are fine stadiums—good for players and spectators.

Maybe they are as hard and true on the surface as lawn tennis courts. When English teams do get beaten on Continental grounds it is paltry to make excuses about the grounds, the size of the ball, and such trifles. Their grounds are the same size as those in England, and if foreigners do use a smaller ball, that is a matter within their discretion. It has never been seen in the international matches. It seems to me that the smaller ball would be good to train with, as it would tend to give greater accuracy when using the larger ball.

CHAPTER XXI

HOW FOOTBALL CONQUERED THE WORLD

SOME seventy years ago those who played Association football in England were generally regarded as harmless lunatics. Men shrugged their shoulders and said: "If they hurt anybody it will only be themselves, and the fewer lunatics the better." That is an impression given me by a man who was enjoying a football frolic when I was a child.

It seems to me as if football has always had detractors and scoffers. Royalty, Parliament, bishops and puritans for centuries tried to prevent the rough revels of parish against parish, when the playing area was a large track of country and town, with a mill-wheel and a church-door, miles apart, as the goals! An encounter of this character would frighten most modern players.

Possibly these rude games were the forerunners of the football that the old-foundation public schools developed according to the size and nature of their playgrounds. All the various rules of these schools were carefully considered by a body of gentlemen at Cambridge University.

These enthusiasts, trying to work out a code that all could play under, whatever may have been their school, produced a set of rules or laws of play that the Football Association, founded in 1863, took as a model for the game they wished to popularize.

It is not necessary to enlarge this summary by details. Suffice it to say that the parent body, as it is now called, gradually evolved the laws under which most civilized nations now play what I like to speak of as "our game."

During the fifty years from 1863 to 1913 this form of football made a great advance and became the national winter game of all Britain. When the F.A. reached its Jubilee year it was decided to celebrate this progress by a banquet in London.

I want readers to know something about this gathering, as it provides evidence of the spread of a pastime that was originally wholly British but was taken up by other countries because they recognized its manly qualities and ready opportunities for sport in our winter, a season of the year when the climate was trying and we had no refreshing recreation for people who could neither hunt nor shoot. Those were the sports of the rich.

Football came and conquered the world because any young man could join in the fun, with but slight demands upon his purse.

As I look at the list of the guests of the Football Association on this occasion, twenty-one years ago, I see that the International Federation of Football Associations, founded in May, 1904, at Paris, sent Baron de Laveleye, of Belgium, one of the founders, to the banquet, and he responded to the toast of that organization, which was a Continental movement in its inception.

Hugo Meisl represented Austria; Professor Hefner, Germany; C.A.W. Hirschman and J. Warner the Netherlands; Adrian Bech, Switzerland; Lieut. E. Kulander and Hugo Vallentin, Sweden; R.M. Peterson, Norway; Nils Middelboe and L. Sylow, Denmark; A.E. Gibbs, Australia and the Commonwealth Association; D.P. Stephenson, Jamaica; and J.O. Anderson and Estlin Grundy, Argentina.

To some, these may be only names, but these men in their different countries or in their homes abroad worked for the good of, and the expansion of the game. Moreover, they show how football, as we understand it, was casting a spell upon youth that had little in common with the Anglo-Saxon race.

Football became a bond of national brotherhood. Britain gave a recreation to the world, a pastime that appealed to all mankind. This was no small achievement, especially when it is remembered that just over forty years ago 'bus and cab drivers derided the country folks who travelled to London to see the Final Tie for the

Association Cup.

Neither Italy nor Spain was represented at that banquet. Nor was Turkey! The allusion to Turkey is not jocular.

About 1913 it was said that if ever the Latin races, particularly Italy and Spain, began to play football in a serious sense, they would surprise the world.

This was the opinion of R.W. Seeldrayers, a barrister, of Brussels, and he was a thoughtful man. His argument was that the Latin races were quick thinkers, swift to act, and clever and daring in any form of exercise that appealed to them.

As for Turkey? Well, I was once told that if anyone ventured to carry a football through the streets of Constantinople he would be apprehended for being in possession of a bomb!

Yet, after the war, about 11 years ago, the Turks began to play football.

Turkey organized a football association, and this was recognized by the government "as an institution of public utility" in January, 1924.

And a few years ago Fred Pagnam, the centre-forward who had played with Liverpool, Arsenal and Watford, was engaged as principal coach by the Turkish Association, who have had their international matches not only with the countries of the Balkans, but with Egypt, Russia, Poland, Estonia, Latvia, Finland, Hungary and Czechoslovakia.

The Turks have lost more matches than they have won, but the day may come when Johnny Turk, as our soldiers called him, may show more facility in the foot-play of the west.

Let us glance at some of the Continental pioneers of football across the English Channel.

As already said, Baron de Lavaleye was one of those who spoke for the International Federation at the Jubilee celebration of the Football Association.

An industrial and commercial magnate of Belgium, he was, in youth, a prominent athlete, and so well preserved was he that at the age of forty he began to teach young Belgians how to play Association football.

When the National Association of Belgium was formed, he became a prominent figure and induced the late King Albert to become interested.

In 1908 England sent a team of amateurs to play Belgium at Brussels. King Albert honoured the match with his presence. At the interval de Laveleye took me across the ground and presented me to His Majesty, who asked many questions. He was curious about the English eleven being exclusively amateur, and said:

"Couldn't you send over a team of amateur and professional players combined?"

I explained that, as a matter of courtesy, since the Belgians were all amateurs, the F.A. had sent a team of their best amateurs.

His Majesty's view was that there should be professionals in every country, and he added: "Their work would be to teach the amateur players and so improve the standard of play."

I also met Count Joseph d'Oultremont, the head of an old and honoured family, who was educated in England and tried to get British games played in Belgium. His sons have also been educated in this country.

Another friend of King Albert, the Count had largely devoted himself to the development of junior football, but he shared His Majesty's views about professionalism.

The Count's opinion was that honest payment for legitimate services was always preferable to veiled professionalism. To that he could never become reconciled.

This nobleman, so well known for his sportsmanship and courtesy, has done much for the game both in Belgium and on the Federation for twenty years.

Both Baron de Laveleye and Count d'Oultremont are still members of the Belgian Association, of which Monsieur Seeldrayers has become the president.

A frequent visitor to England for international matches prior to the European War, Seeldrayers, while studying for the Bar, was a keen player with the Racing Club of Brussels in his youth, and for many years has devoted his leisure to the good government of the game, in Belgium and also as a vice-president and one of the three members of the Emergency Committee of the Federation.

Probably every English player who has been to Belgium will remember Mons. F.A. Konig ("Frank," everyone called him), who out of pure friendliness used to meet every English team on arrival in his country, and in a quiet, unassuming way overcame any difficulties and made their path pleasant.

The Football Association presented him with a gold cigar-case as a gesture of appreciation. To no other honorary guide and adviser has the F.A. expressed gratitude in this way.

Konig said that he was the debtor, for what he knew of "football and sporting spirit" he had learned from English football folk.

The President to-day of the Federation and of the French Association is Mons. Jules Rimet, an astute politician and an orator.

He and I both liked to have Henri Delaunay, the journalist who is the secretary for France, present, as he acted as interpreter of our conversation.

In his early days Delaunay was actively connected with the French Athletic Association, but he thought it would be better to found a distinct organization for football, so as to give more freedom for developments.

In this movement he was joined by M. Charles Simon, with whom I had the most happy relations. The European war took him out of our sight for evermore, but he will be remembered not only as an organizer but as an enthusiast. Mons. René Guérin was the first president of the Federation. France has always been to the fore in this movement.

When peace was restored, Delaunay, who was an able and far-seeing legislator, worked hard for the reconstruction of the Federation, which is now the recognized authority in most parts of the world where the game is played—except Great Britain and her family of nations.

In these days little is heard of Dr. Robert Hefner, but he took a deep and active interest when German football was in its infancy. As a student and later as a professor in one of the leading universities, he was an upholder of amateurism and even adopted the British definition of an amateur. With fair hair and square head, he was a typical German, and at first had a passion to recast the laws of the game. Then he recognized that these laws were the fruits of long experience and was content. He contributed articles to the football year book of the Fatherland. He admired England and English football and adopted the English phrase, "Play the game."

Football, which was highly recommended as a physical aid for youth by the ex-Crown Prince in the long ago, is played all over Germany, where there are seven League Competitions. There is a national championship confined to sixteen clubs from the Leagues and a national cup for representative teams from each League.

Our game has gone ahead in Italy and Spain. The motto of the Italians has been "Always advance." For the last twenty years Italy has consistently developed, and now plays as fine football as any country in Europe. The clubs have had English coaches, and the players have been such apt pupils that it is doubtful if they have any superiors, either individually or collectively.

The International Federation founded a competition called "The World's Cup" that was first played for at Montevideo in 1930. This was won by Uruguay, who defeated Argentina in the final match. In the Argentine eleven there were players of Italian blood and descent.

The second tournament was decided this year in Rome, when the Italian eleven won, and it throws a flood of light on Italy's capacity when it is recalled that they defeated the United States, Spain, Austria and Czechoslovakia.

The Italians never had more than a goal scored against them, and apart from the United States, who were easy victims, the matches were tremendous contests.

Any country, even an all-British eleven, would have been severely taxed to master Spain, Austria, and the Czechs in successive matches on different grounds in various parts of Italy. We know the struggles England has had against these three countries abroad.

If anyone entertains the idea that this comprehensive title of

World Champions has been cheaply won by Italy, it were wise to discard that opinion. All over the Southern Peninsula the game flourishes and is well governed.

Signor Mussolini takes a great personal interest in a game that he holds to be a national asset. For many years I corresponded with Signor Vaccaro, and on the occasions when I met him in Italy I was impressed with his knowledge of the game. Indeed, it seemed as if almost everybody in the country was well acquainted with football.

In Spain good progress has also been made. People in England are inclined to suggest that some nations will never succeed in football because of their temperament, racial defects or impulsive actions. These characteristics have not proved a barrier to success on the field so far as I am aware.

The Spaniards are good players; make no mistake about that. They were not seen at their best in London in 1931.

I was travelling to Glasgow for the Scottish match in April, 1923. At Leeds, just as the train was about to continue the journey, the door of the compartment was opened, a heavy portmanteau was thrown in, and the portly form of a gentleman, a foreigner beyond a doubt, subsided into a seat just as the train moved. When he had recovered normal breathing he leaned forward and said

"You are Mr. Wall?" "Yes," I answered, "and you are Señor Juan Gampa, of the Spanish F.A. I am delighted to meet you under such circumstances and so far from Barcelona."

On a business trip to England, he had "made" time to see the match between Scotland and England.

He became the guest of the F.A., for no one had done more for football in Spain, although he used to breed bulls for the ring. He had, however, an idea that football would eventually undermine the national sport of bull-fighting. The boy, he argued, showed the trend of the times by posing on the playground not as the matador or the picador, but as the centre-forward and the goalkeeper.

Señor Gampa, who was really a Swiss long resident in Spain, did not live to see the strides the game made in his adopted country.

Football has become just as much the sporting heritage of the Continent as of England. I should place Italy, Austria and Germany as the first three in order of merit, but the Belgians, Danes, Norwegians, Swedes and others play quite well, although they are not so strong as those countries which have openly adopted professionalism. The Scandinavian countries have not the same material and scope. They have played football purely as a recreation, and I dare say they are quite as skilful as most of our amateurs.

The young Dutchmen of Holland can put up a good game. We should not forget that the chief executive officer of the International Federation for 25 years was a stockbroker of Amsterdam, Mr. C.A.W. Hirschman, who was clever and very ambitious for the success of the Federation.

Where that was concerned he did not recognize limitations. The Federation was to take the whole of the football world under its wing. When this became clear in 1928, the British associations resigned.

The chief satisfaction to Englishmen is that nearly all these nations have been taught, or coached, by elderly professionals from this country, and that, in the main, they play according to the laws of the game as passed by the International Board of Great Britain, who decided to co-opt the Federation. I wrote "in the main" because, for instance, in some Continental countries they do not charge the goalkeeper at any time.

Some countries would like to introduce substitutes for injured players. This reminds me that in November, 1913, our English amateurs played their brethren from Holland at Hull. The visitors were flying Dutchmen, for they had a dashing set of forwards. Their shooting was weak. England led at half time by a penalty goal, kicked by Arthur Knight, of Portsmouth.

J. Voss, of Utrecht, a clever inside-left, was injured and could not turn out for the second half. Thereupon Vivian Woodward, the English captain, appealed to the International Selection Committee of the F.A. for power to allow Holland to play a substitute. The concession was made, and Westra Van Holthe, of Essen, took the place of Voss.

This was not mere "gallery play" by Woodward, who, by the way, had played at The Hague eight months earlier in the year, when Holland won by 2–1, both their goals being got by H.F. de Groot, of Rotterdam, who was inside-right at Hull.

In the latter half of this match at Hull, Boutmy, the right half-back of Holland, equalized from the white spot, and then it was that Woodward concentrated on the winning goal, which he obtained as the match was drawing to a close.

It is possible that Holland would not have been allowed a substitute if England in 1908 had not granted Wales the privilege of playing Dai Davies, the Bolton Wanderer, in their goal during the second half because L.R. Roose had been injured in the first half. Even Sir Charles Clegg was anxious that Wales should be helped out of the difficulty on that occasion.

I am not in favour of substitutes. Possibly in 1908 and 1913 clubs and countries were not so strict as to-day, but there is a great principle involved. There is a definite law regarding substitutes that must be observed. That law has been seriously thought out, passed and maintained.

Both teams enter the field with a full knowledge of the risks that have to be taken and that if a man is severely injured by risky, reckless or wanton play they may have to be a man short.

There are those who think that if the goalkeeper has to retire another custodian should fill the vacancy.

Not even for a goalkeeper should such a concession be granted.

After all, goalkeepers are just the same as other players. Even if they are the last line of the defence, they have rights exclusively their own, and the backs are there to shoulder off those who wish to charge the 'keeper into the net.

That rarely happens, and if it does, in most cases the guardian of the goal must admit that he has either been at fault in gathering the ball or slower than he ought to have been.

If, before a match, both sides agree to play substitutes, they can do so, but only in a non-competitive game.

CHAPTER XXII

VIEWS AND REFLECTIONS

THERE are two outstanding differences between British and Continental football. The first that comes to mind is that of charging the goalkeeper.

Our law reads:— "The goalkeeper shall not be charged except when he is holding the ball, or obstructing an opponent, or when he has passed outside the goal area."

The match between England and Scotland, at Chelsea's ground in 1913, was decided by the charging of the goalkeeper, for Hampton, the bold Aston Villa centre, who led England's line, so timed his tackle that Brownlie, the Scottish custodian, was forced into the goal with the ball in his hands.

No one grumbled.

Obviously it is the duty of the goalkeeper to rid himself of the ball immediately he either touches or grips it. It is his business to get the ball away. To stop the ball is only half of his job. If he wilfully obstructs an opponent, or wanders outside the rectangle, where he has protection, he becomes subject to the same laws as any other player.

In the recent match in London between England and Italy the referee would not permit the goalkeeper to be charged. It led to misunderstanding. The referees in Italy do not control the game as our officials do. That was the real reason of the Italians' crude play. They would never have attempted to play as they did on many occasions, had they known that they were acting contrary to the laws of the game.

The goalkeeper in England has now a protection that was

denied him in early days. There was a time when one forward would charge the custodian while another man was shooting. The 'keeper had to have one eye on the charge and the other on the ball.

There was no difference between the man in goal and any other player until 1892–93, when it was decided that "the goalkeeper shall not be charged except he be in the act of playing the ball, or is obstructing an opponent."

Two or three seasons later "in the act of playing the ball" was defined as "actual contact with the ball," but in June, 1897, these words were changed to "when he is holding the ball."

In 1902–3 the law was again revised so that the 'keeper had complete protection from charging, except under the three conditions in the wording of the law as it stands at present. The life of the goalkeeper has been made much more bearable.

What I should like Continental countries to grasp is that the custodian has never had absolute relief from being charged, or tackled legitimately, but he is now given reasonable safety, so that he has a chance of both stopping the shot and disposing of the ball.

That is fair, but there are still three conditions in which he may be charged: (1) Holding the ball; (2) obstructing an opponent; and (3) outside his goal area.

If Continental countries and clubs would remember these conditions, their matches, when meeting British teams in the future, would be much more pleasant.

These misinterpretations of the law cause no end of bother on the Continent, but I hold that it is necessary for Great Britain to set a high standard of fair play and to prevail upon the responsible authorities in every country to see that their referees insist upon the laws of the game being obeyed, and that they should be firm in suppressing rough play and ungentlemanly conduct.

Again, there is the permitting of substitutes to take the place of "injured" players. This practice is general on the Continent, whereas the first sentence in the laws of the game reads: "The game shall be played by not more than 11 players on each side."

By arrangement before the start of any match, not played under the rules of a competition, substitutes may be allowed for injured players. But note this decision of the International Board: This law "is binding only on the four British associations with regard to international matches." Therefore substitutes are allowed in international matches on the Continent. As I have said already, I am against this practice.

I was in Paris in November, 1934, when Arsenal, the premier professional club of England, played the Racing Club, the premier professional club of France. It was not a representative contest, and substitutes were played.

During the game four of the Racing Club eleven retired injured, and there were other players ready to take their places. Insufficient time was given to ascertain that the men were really injured, except in one instance, that of the goalkeeper.

From what has come under my observation, I contend that it is essential that substitution of players should not be permitted under any circumstances, that the scheme leads to abuses, and that it has become such a common practice that players are encouraged to leave the field for a mere scratch. A football match should be played by a a men, not by relays of men.

The International Federation of Football Associations have delegates sitting on the International Board. The Federation should enforce the laws that they have assented to.

The Associations of Great Britain who do abide by these laws, are apart from the Federation, and must remain outside their pale, even if we Britons do play games with European countries.

The International Federation is an excellent organization, but too unwieldy. The object of the Federation was to control the world of football. That cannot be done successfully. There is scope enough for any organization in covering European countries. It is a mistake to attempt to legislate for and govern the United States and South America.

But we—that is, the British Associations—whilst retaining our independence, can work in harmony with the Federation for the general good of the game. That is a simple plan for the common weal of football in Europe.

There are changes that I should like to see carried out—the first and foremost being the numbering of the players. Players should wear numbers in all representative matches, Cup ties and League games. That should be a compulsory rule for the benefit of the spectators, who keep football alive and provide the revenue for all associations and clubs.

Even a programme is not an infallible and never-failing guide to the identity of players who are constantly moving, often at considerable speed, and rapidly changing their positions either as attackers or defenders, and often both at the same time.

From my own experience of certain teams, and particularly of many players who have a roving commission and turn up in the most unexpected places, I realize that there is great difficulty in identifying them.

Spectators are constantly asking questions about the name of the man who scored the goal, or who made a very fine pass, or who stepped on the goal line and made a magnificent kick when but for his foresight and accurate play, the goal would have fallen.

Apart from these incidents of the game, remember that a figure on the back of a man's jersey is as ready an index and an aid as the numbers on the back of a motor-car.

In all matches there is a visiting team who are comparative strangers to sightseers who only know their own club eleven. There are thousands of spectators who have no knowledge of either side.

In large cities there is always a big floating population and visitors from other centres, especially if the game is likely to be an exciting contest. They are attracted and have as much right to what ought to be common knowledge as the residents or followers of the clubs.

The Final Tie for the Cup every spring attracts thousands of people who do not know either team well enough to identify the players at a distance, and many come from the distant places of the earth; Britons home on leave as well as foreigners. They have no means of knowing who's who. And the same doubt and confusion arises at international matches.

Then there seems to be some desire to increase the number of officials who control a match. There are advocates of a referee for each half of the field, and for goal judges—a title coined for men who would stand behind the net and presumably decide whether the whole ball has been over the line.

With a little ingenuity more officials could be created. Why not linesmen for each half and men to stand at each corner flag to adjudicate upon nice points that may arise. In my opinion it would be a great blunder to multiply officials and interfere with the spirit and intentions of the laws as applied to the referee.

These suggestions are due either to the assumption that referees are not as competent as formerly or that clubs have become terrified of the possibilities attending a mistake by a referee.

Years ago a famous club lost the opportunity of returning to the First Division owing to the decision of a referee that disallowed a goal held to be perfectly legitimate. That decision kept the club in the Second Division for another season. The club said very little about the misfortune. Perhaps other clubs have not been so tolerant.

I have occasionally heard that it is the practice of some referees to tell their linesmen that their sole duty is to signal when the ball is over the touchline: "Leave everything to me, except when the ball goes out of play." If the three officials co-operate most fully, as they can, within the law, there will be few miscarriages of justice.

There was a time when there were no referees; when the captains decided matters in dispute. Some of our friends would describe that era as the halcyon days of amateurism!

Then it was that reports of matches concluded with such words as those: "Result: The Optimists won by two goals and a disputed goal to one goal for the Pessimists."

Referees there must be, but neither in numbers nor big fees can safety from error be assured.

There have been, there are, and there always will be, some men who use their talents, energies and influence for the sake of the game, so they say, but whose motives are, in fact, not so disinterested. This is regrettable. It is not in the best interests of sport that sham amateurism, for instance, should be possible, or countenanced either on the field of play or in the legislative chamber.

This principle is one which should be carefully considered by the Football Association and by the associations of all nationalities. In view of entanglements which may develop, and, I fear, will prove harmful to football, this safeguarding principle should be made applicable to all governing authorities.

This, I venture to suggest, is obvious to others beside myself.

In closing, let me say that I entirely disapprove of the tendency to depart from the old formation of teams.

As soon as the off-side law was revised—one of the best alterations ever made, for it has reduced useless stoppages of play by 75 per cent—players began to think about what they called W and other formations.

It is nice to see them thinking about the game and making experiments. New ideas are welcome, but they must be examined and tested.

To introduce quarter-backs, half-backs and a three-quarter-back into Association football is, however, in my opinion a big mistake.

Stand firm by the old formation, unless another James comes into the world to gather stray balls, and make the most of the larger freedom given to forwards, thus enabling them to support each other for the benefit of the team.